Policing, Surveillance and Social Control

Policing, Surveillance and Social Control

CCTV and police monitoring of suspects

Tim Newburn and Stephanie Hayman

WILLAN
PUBLISHING

Published by

Willan Publishing
Culmcott House
Mill Street, Uffculme
Cullompton, Devon
EX15 3AT, UK
Tel: +44(0)1884 840337
Fax: +44(0)1884 840251
e-mail: info@willanpublishing.co.uk
website: www.willanpublishing.co.uk

Published simultaneously in the USA and Canada by

Willan Publishing
c/o ISBS, 5824 N.E. Hassalo St
Portland, Oregon 97213-3644, USA
Tel: +001(0)503 287 3093
Fax: +001(0)503 280 8832
website: www.isbs.com

First published 2002

ISBN 1-903240-50-6 (cased)

British Library Cataloguing-in-Publication Data

A catalogue record for this book is available from the British Library.

Typeset by PDQ Typesetting, Newcastle-under-Lyme, Staffordshire

Printed and bound by T J International Ltd, Trecerus Industrial Estate, Padstow, Cornwall

Contents

List of illustrations

Acknowledgements

As with all enterprises of this nature there are numerous people to whom we are indebted. Thanks are due to Dr Gary Slapper of the Open University who first put us in touch with the proposed experiment at Kilburn. We are grateful to Chief Superintendent Paul Green for inviting us to undertake the evaluation, for giving us access to staff and records and for commenting on the final product. Our time at Kilburn was both facilitated and supported by Chief Inspector Peter King. He was unfailingly helpful. The study was supported by a grant from the Nuffield Foundation. We are grateful to them for their support and in particular to Sharon Witherspoon who was understanding and patient when elements of the study proved trickier, and more time-consuming, than we had at first anticipated.

The first phase of the fieldwork was undertaken by Dr Oliver Phillips, now of Keele University. His good humour, enthusiasm and research skills got the project off to a flying start and the study would not have been nearly as successful without his input. Simon Shaw spent more time than was undoubtedly good for him poring over police custody records and we would like to record our thanks to him. Julie Latreille 'punched' the data for us with her customary efficiency and Mike Shiner applied his considerable skills to the resulting dataset and guided us towards what was (and away from what was not) meaningful.

We would like to thank all those who gave time for interviews or who provided information in other ways. In particular, thanks are due to members of the Marlon Downes Trust, members of the Brent Police and Community Consultative Group and Molly Meacher, of the Police Complaints Authority, all of whom agreed to lengthy interviews. Inspector Oonagh Vyse offered kindly support at all stages. The police officers and prisoners at Kilburn tolerated the presence of researchers with grace, often in circumstances when they might have preferred to be alone. This study would not have been possible in its final form without their assistance. Both Clive Norris and Nick Tilley read the book in draft at short notice and made some perceptive and useful comments. We are grateful to both.

Our families had to cope with the pressures imposed by an intensive period of writing. We acknowledge this with gratitude.

Chapter 1

Background

Deaths can be public or private: deaths in police custody, by their very nature, are secret and enclosed tragedies.

(Benn and Worpole 1986: 78)

Introduction

Allegedly, we live in 'New Times'. Post-Fordist means of production, the emergence of new technologies, particularly communications technologies, have led to a profound restructuring of the late modern world. There has been a significant shift towards the privatisation of public space, as well as radical changes to the organisation of urban environments and to the sources of identity formation. According to Giddens (1990) the disembedding of social activity from localised contexts, and the changing of sources of trust from localised systems to abstract systems, has resulted in a heightening of what he terms 'ontological insecurity'. Correlatively, security has become 'commodified' (Jones and Newburn 1998) and new technologies of surveillance, particularly closed-circuit television (CCTV), have become increasingly prominent as the means of governing particular (especially public) spaces. Such technologies have enabled the emergence of a form of 'digital rule' (Jones 2000), where 'at a distance monitoring' becomes a key element in electronic crime control.

Criminologists have been much taken by these new technologies. Hitherto, however, their gaze has rested primarily on the impact of such technologies on public space, and has been characterised by a somewhat dystopian view of such developments. This book focuses on the experimental introduction of CCTV within a rather different form of 'space': a custody suite within a busy police station in Kilburn in North London. The cameras, placed in the reception area, the corridors between the cells, and in all of the cells in the suite, were designed to monitor continuously the behaviour of people in custody. As such, the experiment provides a marked departure from many, if not most, previous uses of CCTV within the fields of criminal justice and crime control. Consequently, it allows us to view the nature and impact of the use of such technology within a very different environment from those where it has previously been studied and, more particularly, brings into focus new questions and issues.

This book is divided into three main parts. In this chapter we consider the background to the experiment in general. We look at the issue of police–community relations and the treatment of suspects in custody. More particularly we consider the problem of deaths in custody and the response of the Police Complaints Authority – a body which has increasingly come to recommend the limited use of electronic surveillance in custody. We provide a brief history of CCTV and conclude by looking at the history of the introduction of the cameras in Kilburn police station (henceforward the 'Kilburn experiment'). Chapter 2 outlines the Kilburn experiment, including how it was presented to staff, to the public, what in general terms it consisted of and how much it cost. Chapter 3 describes the setting for the experiment: the custody suite. How does the suite operate? And just who is kept in custody during the course of a year and a half in the life of a police station? We examine the backgrounds of all suspects held in cells: their sex, age, ethnic and cultural backgrounds, together with periods of time held in custody, medical and drug issues, and strip searches.

The second section in the book looks at the experiment in practice. Chapter 4 considers the novel position of the gaolers and custody sergeants responsible for monitoring suspects. In all, 29 officers were interviewed before or after the installation of the cell cameras. How do they feel about this work and its impact on their jobs? Of course, these officers are subject to surveillance themselves, as the cameras are located not just in the cells but also in the reception area and thoroughfares of the custody suite. What are their experiences of the impact of the cameras on privacy, safety and rights? Chapter 5 examines the experience of electronic surveillance from the point of view of the main group being watched: those held in custody. Based on interviews with 73 suspects, again conducted both before and after installation of the cell cameras, we explore their knowledge of the cameras and their experience of the impact of cameras on privacy, protection, safety and rights. Chapter 6 examines the experiences of those 'mediating' individuals and agencies that also work within the custody suite: appropriate adults, forensic medical examiners, lay visitors, and solicitors. How do they view the impact of the introduction of cameras on police officers, on suspects, and on themselves?

The final section of the book draws the previous sections together and locates these arguments within broader debates about surveillance: the nature and uses of risk in relation to policing and social control; the management of subject populations; and the implications of the experiment for the governance of the police. Much social scientific consideration of CCTV is dystopian in character, focusing primarily on the negative, intrusive face of surveillance. In our view not only does electronic surveillance have 'two faces' – one that intrudes and impacts on privacy, and one that watches and, potentially, protects – but both may be visible simultaneously. We conclude by arguing that if one wishes to understand properly the nature and impact of electronic surveillance then, as the Kilburn experiment illustrates, it is important to focus on both faces of CCTV.

For reasons we outline later in this chapter, the use of CCTV to monitor prisoners in police custody is likely to increase in the future. For that reason, among others, the Kilburn experiment is likely to prove of great interest to police forces throughout England and Wales and, indeed, elsewhere. In a postscript, therefore, we offer some practical suggestions for the future use of CCTV in custody suites.

Police–community relations and the treatment of suspects in custody

The criminal justice system has always given some official body the power to inquire into offences and to question suspects. Originally these powers were conferred on juries, with the police taking over the role of investigating offences in the first half of the nineteenth century. For as long as the police have had powers of detention for the purposes of questioning there have been concerns about the treatment and welfare of people in custody in police stations. From 1912 up until the early 1980s, police powers were governed by 'Judges' Rules', a non-statutory statement of principles and practice which set out what the police could do when 'they were endeavouring to discover the author of a crime' (Judge 1986: 176). There were, however, important gaps in the Rules, and their legal status was unclear. By the late 1970s, as a result of this and concern about apparent miscarriages of justice, criticism was growing about the treatment of suspects in custody.

A number of high profile cases focused particular attention on the care and treatment of suspects in custody. One of the first concerned a young man, Stephen McCarthy, arrested in Islington in November 1970 after a violent confrontation. Allegedly assaulted by police officers during his arrest, McCarthy's condition deteriorated during the seven weeks he spent in custody in Wormwood Scrubs and Dover Borstal (Benn and Worpole 1986) and he was admitted to hospital in early January 1971 with violent headaches and vomiting. He went into a coma and died on 26 January. The subsequent inquest brought in a verdict of 'death by natural causes' but noted that there had been insufficient care given at Wormwood Scrubs. McCarthy's family and friends, convinced that there had been a serious miscarriage of justice, mounted a vigorous campaign. Demands for a public inquiry fell on deaf ears despite the vociferous public protests. As Benn and Worpole note:

> The march to the police station [in Islington]; disbelieving outbursts in court; the repeated calls for a Public Inquiry that are then peremptorily dismissed; the demonstrations and unnecessary, sometimes violent arrests; all these elements of the McCarthy case were to be repeated in subsequent years with increasingly serious political consequences.
>
> (1986: 18)

The death of Liddle Towers in 1976 is a clear illustration of this point. Towers, aged 39 at the time, was arrested outside a nightclub in Gateshead early in 1976. Eyewitnesses alleged that he was severely beaten by the eight arresting officers. He was kept in the police station overnight and then released but 'was so ill and badly injured that he could hardly move' (Scraton and Chadwick 1987b: 72). Towers died three weeks after his arrest. No police officers were prosecuted, no breach of force discipline was held to have taken place and the subsequent inquest returned a verdict of 'justifiable homicide'. The Attorney General later applied to have the verdict quashed on the grounds that it was inconsistent with the evidence. A second inquest returned a verdict of 'death by misadventure', having been instructed by the coroner that this would be possible even if during the course of the arrest 'there were some acts which went beyond the bounds of proper conduct on the part of police officers' (Scraton and Chadwick 1987a: 216).

Perhaps the most notorious of all the causes célèbres was that concerning the death of Blair Peach. A schoolteacher, Blair Peach was part of an Anti-Nazi League demonstration against a meeting of the

National Front in Southall in West London in 1979. The demonstration became violent and a large number of people were injured. Peach, allegedly on his way home from the demonstration, was caught in a police charge by the Special Patrol Group. He sustained massive injuries to his head, including a fractured skull, and died within minutes. Though not a death in police custody, or where custody was involved at all, the death of Blair Peach further focused attention on problematic police–community relations, on police violence, and on the difficulties in securing any form of official condemnation of police action. After another highly controversial inquest, a verdict of 'death by misadventure' was returned.

Later in the same year a death in custody resulted in a case that went all the way to the European Court. Once again a man being arrested was, as recounted by civilian eyewitnesses, given a severe beating. Jimmy Kelly, the man in question, was both drunk and disorderly at the time of his arrest, according to the officers concerned. The officers who first approached Kelly admitted employing violent tactics to restrain him and 'one policeman admitted to sitting on him and punching him "three or four times" in the stomach' (Scraton and Chadwick 1987b: 81). He remained disorderly and was restrained by one officer standing on his feet and another kneeling on his chest (he had already hurt his head falling out of a police car). He was transported to the police station semi-conscious on the floor of a transit van, was dropped on his head at the police station, and left unconscious on the floor. He died in custody.

The case became a focus for a confrontation between critics of the police and the police establishment itself. The Chief Constable of Merseyside, Kenneth Oxford, said that the case was used to mount an 'almost neurotic attack on the police service generally' and the chairman of the Police Federation described the campaign to highlight the perceived injustices as 'the usual ragbag of people who spend their time sniping at the police service' (Scraton and Chadwick 1987a: 219).

Two MPs, Michael Meacher and Stan Newens, laid questions in Parliament in a bid to get information about the numbers and causes of deaths in custody. At the time no central record of deaths in custody existed and the data had to be gathered from all forces in England and Wales individually. According to the eventual answer, a total of 274 people died whilst in police custody between 1970 and 1979. Of these, 138 died in police cells and 136 in hospital but while still in police custody. In 1980 a House of Commons Home Affairs Select Committee (HAC) inquiry was established to consider deaths in custody. Those giving evidence were confined largely to police groups and other official bodies, such as the Coroners' Society and the British Association for Forensic Medicine. The only likely critical voice was that of Meacher, and Scraton and Chadwick (1987a: 217) conclude that 'what was claimed as a thorough HAC inquiry, then, was by the very constitution of the evidence little more than a summary of "official discourse" '. The report dismissed 'generalised accusations of police brutality to those in custody' and went on to state that 'the limits of our investigation do not permit us to form any view about individual allegations' (1987a: 217–18).

These and other cases (James Davey, Richard 'Cartoon' Campbell, Jim Heather-Hayes, Colin Roach and Helen Smith) highlighted major worries about the lack of safeguards covering suspects held in police custody. At approximately the same time, but from a different angle, a series of major 'miscarriages of justice' was also raising concerns about the behaviour and standards of the police. Doubts about the convictions of the 'Guildford Four' and the 'Birmingham Six', among many others, again focused attention on the way in which suspects were treated in custody; specifically in such cases concerning how confessions were elicited. Indeed, according to Rose (1996: 119) 'the case of the Guildford Four destroyed what was left of the old regime in criminal justice. Its effect on public and judicial attitudes was electrifying, but the regime had already been terminally undermined by two pieces of legislation'. The first of these was the Police and Criminal Evidence Act 1984 (PACE).[1]

A Royal Commission was established in the aftermath of the wrongful conviction of three youths for the murder of Maxwell Confait. The Royal Commission on Criminal Procedure was to 'have regard both to the interests of the community in bringing offenders to justice and to the rights and liberties of persons suspected or accused of crime' (RCCP 1981: iv). The Commission, which reported in 1981, made far-reaching recommendations that sought to establish a balance between the rights of suspects and the powers of the police. One of the outcomes was PACE, which provided a detailed legislative framework for the operation of police powers and for the protection of suspects' rights (superseding the Judges' Rules).

In fact, PACE both increased police powers and introduced a new system of safeguards. It created a new type of police officer – the 'custody officer' – on whom responsibility rests for the protection of the rights of suspects and who is independent of the investigation of the crime. PACE, and its associated *Codes of Practice*, set out how suspects are to be treated. Arrested suspects must be 'booked in' by custody officers, and must be informed of their rights, both orally and by giving them a notice in writing. PACE *Codes of Practice* make a number of stipulations about the conditions of detention in the police station. These cover standards of physical comfort, provision of refreshments, detention of juveniles, use of reasonable force and the frequency of visits to check on welfare. Custody officers must call a police surgeon immediately if a detainee appears to be physically or mentally ill, injured, unconscious or semi-conscious, behaving abnormally or otherwise in need of medical attention. The detainee need not request attention, although if they do the surgeon must be called as soon as practicable. The custody officer has to pay special regard to the needs of 'vulnerable prisoners' such as the mentally handicapped and mentally disordered, to juveniles in general and to those for whom English is not a first language.

One of the areas in which there was considerable and specific concern at the time of the Royal Commission on Criminal Procedure, was the interrogation of suspects. PACE sought to introduce a series of provisions that would minimise the risk of false or unreliable confessions. These covered the length of time suspects could be detained without charge, limits over the appearance of 'third parties' during interview, the presence of an 'appropriate adult' for vulnerable suspects and regulations over the length and timing of interviews. Prior to the introduction of PACE there were frequent disputes over whether suspects had actually made the confessions in the terms alleged by the police. To begin to address this, in the early 1980s the Home Office held trials in which police interviews with suspects were tape-recorded (Willis 1984; Willis, Macleod and Naish 1988) and, subsequently, the PACE *Codes of Practice* stipulated that interviews should take place in an interview room which should have tamper-proof tape-recording facilities and that the whole of the interview should be recorded.

The importance of this for present purposes is the parallel it has with some of the issues arising in relation to the proposal to introduce CCTV in custody suites. Early police views of tape-recording were sceptical and some research has suggested that one of the consequences of PACE has been to shift 'unwanted behaviour' elsewhere. Thus, research suggests that some officers avoid the constraints of tape-recorded interrogations in a minority of cases by conducting interviews outside the police station or before or after formal interrogations, such as in 'welfare' visits to the custody suite (Dixon *et al.* 1990; McConville *et al.* 1991). The continued shortcomings of tape-recorded interviewing have led some to recommend the introduction of videotaping of interrogations, though the Royal Commission on Criminal Justice (RCCJ 1993) suggested further research was required. However, the RCCJ did recommend that a permanent CCTV camera should be placed in the custody suites of police stations in order to reduce malpractice associated with non-tape-recorded interviewing of suspects.

PACE was the subject of vociferous criticism at the time of its passage, and critics continue to scrutinise its limitations. There is considerable criminological debate over whether or not the changes it introduced represented a 'sea change' in the treatment of detained suspects (Dixon 1991; Sanders 1997). Despite this ongoing debate, PACE is widely accepted by commentators as representing a major step forward in relation to the rights of people detained in police stations. Indeed, safeguards for suspects contained in the Act go considerably beyond what is available in many other European countries (Morgan 1996). Reiner (2000: 176), the most distinguished commentator on these matters, describes PACE as 'the single most significant landmark in the modern development of police powers' and suggests that, overall, it 'seems to have had a profound effect on the nature and outcomes of police handling of suspects' (p. 180).

What is known about deaths in custody?

The most comprehensive research on deaths in custody was carried out for the Home Office Police Research Group in the late 1990s (Leigh *et al.* 1998). The authors studied all deaths in police custody between 1990 and 1996 (excluding those where the police presence was deemed to be 'tangential') – a total of 277 deaths. Of these, they found that the overwhelming majority of those that died were white (87 per cent), male (92 per cent) and aged between 20 and 50 (74 per cent) reflecting, the authors believed, the general characteristics of the custodial population.[2] Most of these detainees had been arrested for 'relatively minor' offences (Leigh *et al.* 1998: 9): 49 per cent for being drunk (drunk and disorderly; drunk and incapable; or drinking and driving); 11 per cent for theft (shoplifting etc.) and 9 per cent on a warrant, a place of safety order or under the Mental Health Act.

In terms of the 'causes' of deaths in custody, they were categorised into three groups: those resulting from the deceased's own actions; those resulting from the deceased's medical condition; and those in which 'another person's actions may have been associated' with the death. Overall, the 275[3] cases were classified as shown in Table 1.1.

Table 1.1. Causal factors: deaths in police custody 1990–1996

	Number	**Per cent**
Deceased's own actions		
Deliberate self-harm (in custody)	76	28
Deliberate self-harm (pre-custody)	17	6
Substance abuse (alcohol)	45	16
Substance abuse (drugs)	16	6
Substance abuse (drugs and alcohol)	8	3
Accident (whilst police present)	10	4
Total	**172**	**63**
Deceased's medical condition		
Heart problems	32	12
Head	27	10
Lung problems	8	3
Epilepsy	4	1
Liver problems	3	1
Miscellaneous	7	3
Total	**81**	**29**
Another person's actions may have been associated		
Police actions	16	6
Doctor's or medic's actions	3	1
Other person's actions	3	1
Total	**22**	**8**
Total	**275**	

Source: Home Office Police Research Group

As can be seen, the single most common cause of death was 'deliberate self-harm' – accounting for almost one-third of cases. A further half of deaths in custody were classified as resulting either from substance misuse or from particular medical conditions. Cases in which the actions of others (police officers, doctors or other medical examiners, others in custody) accounted for only 8 per cent of cases (22 cases in all). The research considered whether any differences could be identified in the nature of deaths in custody according to the ethnicity of detainees. The number of cases was not large enough to provide statistically significant results. Nonetheless, some differences were still noted. In summary, these were that:

- a smaller proportion of black than white detainees were arrested for alcohol-related offences;
- a larger proportion of black than white detainees were arrested for drugs-related offences;
- a greater proportion of white than black detainees died from in-custody deliberate self-harm or from medical conditions;
- over one-third of cases in which a black detainee died occurred in circumstances in which police actions may have been a factor (the proportion rises to almost one-half if the cases of accidental death where the police were present are added) – this compared with only 4 per cent of cases where the detainee was white.

In terms of the lessons to be learned, the authors described in some detail actions that needed to be taken in relation to health and behaviour checks of detainees, careful and accurate maintenance of records, and modifications in the use of restraint techniques. They recommended medical training for civilian and officer custody staff, and the use of detoxification and drying-out facilities rather than police custody for some detainees. Finally, they recommended careful examination of the use of CCTV in custody suites, including in one or two cells designated for 'at risk' detainees,[4] though they noted that in 23 of the cases in the sample CCTV was in place (though it was unclear precisely where).

The Police Complaints Authority

Despite the improvements that it is generally agreed have been instituted in the treatment of suspects since the passage of PACE, concerns remain. In particular, in some communities suspicions about the treatment of suspects in police stations remain high and, despite the protection in place, incidents of injury, (self-) harm and, occasionally, death still occur. Indeed, until relatively recently the numbers of deaths in police custody had been rising – from approximately 20 a year in the late 1970s to a high point of 65 in 1999. Particular concern was focused on the issue by the apparently steep rise in deaths in police care or custody in the three years prior to 1999, though there was then a very significant drop in the subsequent year (see Figure 1.1).

Figure 1.1 Deaths in police care or custody 1996–2000

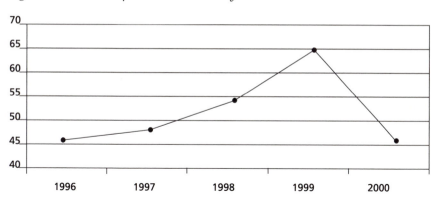

A threefold categorisation of the causes of these deaths is provided by the Police Complaints Authority (PCA). This distinguishes between deaths from 'apparent suicide', 'alcohol and/or drugs', and 'medical/ natural causes/other'. It is not entirely clear what 'other' refers to in the third category. A breakdown of the deaths in custody according to this classification is provided in Figure 1.2.

Figure 1.2 Causes of deaths in police care or custody 1997–1999

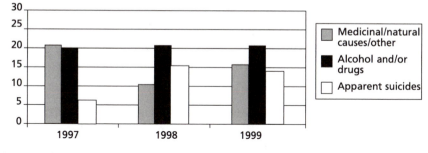

Source: Police Complaints Authority, 1999

As a response to these trends, and the subsequent concern, the PCA held a conference in October 1998 entitled 'Deaths in Police Custody: Reducing the Risks'. It later published a report of the same name (PCA 1999) in which it set out recommendations resulting from the conference. More particularly, the Authority stated:

Not all deaths which occur in police custody result from actions at the point of arrest or detention of the individual. However, it would appear that some deaths could have been prevented had alternative

11

accommodation, improved management and training or other changes to the system been in place.

(http://www.pca.gov.uk/news/deaths2.htm)

In his remarks accompanying the publication of the Report, the then Chairman of the PCA, Sir Peter Moorhouse, drew particular attention to the disproportionate number of Black and Asian people that died in police custody. He suggested that the key to reduction of deaths in police custody lay in early identification of those 'who are vulnerable, either because of physical or mental conditions and maintaining a close watch on their well-being' (PCA press release, 8 July 1999). During the previous year the PCA had investigated the deaths of suspects in custody in Cambridge, Cheltenham, Colchester, Crawley, Gwent, Hull, Leeds, Plumstead, Rawtenstall, Smethwick, and Swansea among others (PCA 1998), and this led the Authority to call for improved training of custody staff, improved cell design to reduce suicide risks and the extension of CCTV to cover 'observation cells' (for 'at risk' suspects).

The PCA conference on Deaths in Police Custody, highlighted three major areas of concern: suicide and self-harm; drug and alcohol misuse; and restraint methods, and again led to calls for the expansion of CCTV in custody suites to include observation cells for particularly vulnerable detainees. The particular concerns were as follows:

Restraint: A struggle between police officers and a detainee may involve the use of manual or mechanical restraints, baton strikes or CS spray. Such deaths (two to three per year) disproportionately involve minority ethnic detainees (www.pca.gov.uk/news.deaths.htm). The PCA recommended that:

- officer training on the dangers of neckholds, and of restraining people face down on the ground with their arms handcuffed behind their backs, should both be reinforced in all self-defence training courses;

- that where officers are involved in the detention of someone under the Mental Health Act 1983 they ensure, wherever possible, that a family member or professional person known to the individual is called to the scene to assist in removing the person to hospital or elsewhere.

Suicide: The majority of such cases involve some form of ligature attached to a fixture either inside the cell or through the cell hatch. Removal of clothing from detainees (allowed under PACE) can be seen as harassment under some circumstances. The PCA therefore recommended:

- improved ventilation of cells in order to allow hatches to be kept closed at all times;

- risk assessment through the asking of standardised questions of detainees during 'booking in';

- appropriately trained nurses to be on call to undertake assessments, liaise with psychiatrists and advise police surgeons and custody sergeants;

- CCTV to be installed in one or two cells in designated custody suites for benefit of vulnerable detainees; and

- 'at risk' detainees, identified at booking in or from records, to be kept under constant supervision using CCTV or civilian staff until their mental state is fully assessed.

Drug or alcohol abuse: Many people are detained in custody because they are drunk. The majority of such arrestees spend some time asleep in a police cell and are discharged without incident. Both the PCA and the Police Federation, however, are of the view that arresting and locking up habitually drunk people is 'totally unsatisfactory' (PCA 1999). PACE *Codes of Practice* require that a detainee who is drunk be roused and spoken to every half hour. However, the *Codes of Practice* are vague and the PCA recommended:

- revisions to the *Codes of Practice* to clarify the actions to be taken in rousing a prisoner, with a clear duty to record the responses of an 'at risk' detainee following each visit;

- further revisions to require that detainees that may have taken Class A drugs be regularly visited and roused;

- improved training of police surgeons, and adoption of a 'consciousness scale' by surgeons and custody officers to enable clear communication about vulnerable prisoners to take place; and

- training for custody officers on the care of detainees who appear to abuse alcohol or drugs.

In its 1996/7 Annual Report the PCA said that 'urgent consideration should be given to extending [CCTV] to cover a small number of cells so that people who are known to pose particular risks could be kept under constant observation' (PCA 1997). As we have already noted, the 1999 PCA Report on reducing the risks of deaths in custody reinforced this, recommending, 'CCTV coverage of custody suites should be expanded to include one or two observation cells for particularly vulnerable detainees' (1999: 17). In making this recommendation the PCA used the example of a custody unit in Exeter which introduced a CCTV system in two cells used for drunk and other vulnerable detainees, as well as in the reception area and the cell corridors. They outlined the benefits of this system as including:

- enabling early intervention in self-harm attempts;

- allowing for constant supervision of vulnerable detainees;

- ensuring the safety of staff, who can monitor detainees without cell entry in appropriate circumstances;

- assisting assessment of detainees.

Although the technology has been available for some time, and cameras had increasingly been used in the charge desk and cell corridor areas of custody suites, concerns about privacy, and civil liberties more generally, inhibited moves to install cameras in the cells themselves. By the time of its follow-up report one year later (PCA 2000), the PCA found that eleven police forces had installed in-cell CCTV cameras in one or more cells. One force, Dorset, had cameras in each of its custody suites, and Devon and Cornwall was to be in a similar position by March 2000. Some forces were piloting cameras, others had plans for future installation. Only one force, Merseyside, had rejected the idea and instead planned to install remote means of checking prisoner's breathing (a cell-breathing monitor) once it had been developed. The Merseyside force's concerns about CCTV were twofold. Firstly, they doubted that a busy custody sergeant would have time to monitor the screens continuously and that, secondly, where a vulnerable prisoner was identified, someone would be assigned to monitor them. Only one force, South Wales, raised concerns about civil liberties though, as the PCA noted, 'this does not imply that other forces are ignoring this issue but most police forces believe the infringement of personal liberty to be outweighed by the greater safety provided to the most vulnerable detainees' (2000: 9).

Concluding its report, the PCA (2000) drew attention to the case of *McCann and Others* v. *the United Kingdom* in the European Court of Human Rights.[5] This ruling on the scope of Article 2 (the right to life) made it clear that police forces were under a duty to improve systems that have failed to protect life in the past, and that forces failing to do this or to provide adequate training for officers, systems and medical care for the preservation of life of incapacitated prisoners may be exposed to legal action under the Human Rights Act. The PCA suggested, *inter alia*, that forces should pay particular attention to the evaluation report of the Devon and Cornwall CCTV scheme and that custody officers should receive clear guidance about the use and monitoring of in-cell CCTV.[6]

A brief history of CCTV

What we are witnessing today...is something like 'safety over-load'...Once collectivities cease to erect and service the city walls and moats, each single resident of the city must attend karate courses.
(Bauman 1999: 49–50)

Bauman's observation concerns what he sees to be the contemporary search for safety in an unsafe world. A search, moreover, aided and abetted by governments that seek to deny their relative impotence by utilising ever more punitive measures and strategies. One such strategy has concerned the spread of electronic surveillance. Partly as a consequence, within the fast-expanding private security industry, the sector that has been growing the quickest is that dealing in the manufacture, installation and monitoring of electronic surveillance equipment (Jones and Newburn 1998). Despite this, there is a tendency in much discussion of private security to focus, if not exclusively, then very significantly upon the 'manned guarding' sector: private security employees (male and female) employed to guard what is usually private or quasi-private property. It is important to keep in mind that the 'private security sector' is a very broad, multi-functional set of industries. Indeed, the proliferation of the use of CCTV in public spaces in the UK is something that distinguishes domestic crime control from the majority of other developed economies (De Waard 1999; Graham *et al.* 1996).

Video technology first appeared in the 1960s and was used, albeit sparingly, fairly early on as a means of apprehending and deterring shoplifters. According to Norris and Armstrong (1999: 35) 'while the technology of mass video surveillance became available from the early 1970s, the political climate retarded its introduction'. The spread of local CCTV systems required support from both central and local government. The metropolitan councils in particular in the 1970s and on into the 1980s remained hostile to CCTV, initially on ideological grounds and later on practical and financial grounds. At the same time, successive Conservative administrations from 1979 played out their distrust of local government in a number of ways, of which one of the more minor was to resist pressure to facilitate local political involvement in the management and direction of crime prevention. By the mid-1980s, however, there was considerable pressure on the state to spread the responsibility for crime control (Garland 1996).

The apparent ubiquitousness of CCTV makes it easy to forget how recent this development has been. The first major city centre CCTV systems were introduced as part of the Safer Cities initiative in the mid-1980s, and a small number of towns went ahead with such installations at around the same time using local authority rather than central government funding. By the mid-1990s fewer than 80 towns and cities had CCTV schemes (Fyfe and Bannister 1996). The spread since then has been so rapid and all-encompassing that one set of commentators has suggested that it is 'now the rule rather than the exception for any reasonably sized community to have CCTV surveillance of its public spaces' (Williams and Johnstone 2000: 184). By May 1999 there were over 530 town and city centre CCTV systems in operation, and further funding has been announced since then.

A number of factors made such a transformation possible. Firstly, and as has been implied, local authorities shifted relatively swiftly from a position of determined resistance to one in which they competed energetically for central government funding for CCTV systems. The reasons for this are undoubtedly complex but include rising local crime rates, declining faith in the formal criminal justice system, and a growing political and ideological emphasis on inter-agency and partnership working. This was most fully articulated at the time by the Morgan Committee – an inquiry established by the Standing Conference on Crime Prevention. Home Office Circular 44/90 had been accompanied by a booklet entitled *Partnership in Crime Prevention* which contained examples of crime prevention initiatives and some examples of good practice. The booklet led indirectly to the establishment of the Morgan Committee, whose terms of reference were to: 'consider and monitor the progress made in the local delivery of crime prevention through the multi-agency or partnership approach, in the light of the guidance in the booklet *Partnership in Crime Prevention* and to make recommendations for the future'. The Morgan Committee's final report (Standing Conference on Crime Prevention 1991) contained nineteen major recommendations. Key among them was that a statutory responsibility on local authorities (alongside the police) should be introduced for the 'stimulation of community safety and crime prevention programmes, and for progressing at a local level a multi-agency approach to community safety'. Though the recommendation was not acted on by a government still distrustful of local councils, it did contribute to a process that led some seven years later to the passage of the Crime and Disorder Act.

Although a decade or so earlier there had been little acceptance within local government of responsibility for crime prevention (Crawford 1997), by the time of the Morgan Report, community safety departments and officers had become relatively commonplace within local government. In 1990 the Association of Metropolitan Authorities published a framework document in which they called for a statutory responsibility for crime prevention to be given to local councils (AMA 1990). The AMA argued that 'the absence of elected members from crime prevention structures may have the effect of marginalising crime prevention from local political issues. Any meaningful local structure for crime prevention must relate to the local democratic structure' (quoted in Crawford 1997: 39). Simultaneously, and importantly, the emergence of a new punitive bipartisan consensus was developing within central government (Garland 2001). The previous two decades had been characterised by considerable ideological differences between the two main parties in relation to crime control. The long process of modernisation of the Labour Party in the 1990s led to a reorientation in relation to crime and justice and, more particularly, to an escalation in punitive rhetoric and an increasing desire to be seen as the 'toughest' on crime issues.

Against this background CCTV might anyway have expanded at a rapid rate. However, it was given further impetus as a result of the broadcast of electronic images taken at a Merseyside shopping centre of the 'moment' at which 2-year-old James Bulger was abducted. As Norris and Armstrong (1999: 37) comment, 'even if CCTV had not saved the toddler, at least it contributed to the identification of the killers'. It also led politicians to suggest, without apparent fear of contradiction, that CCTV 'works'. Indeed, despite what was, at best, mixed research evidence (Burrows 1979; Poyner 1988, 1992), politicians both national and local rushed to proclaim the virtues of the closed-circuit television camera. Moreover, it appeared that they were pushing against an open door, for the British 'public' appeared similarly keen on CCTV and were apparently unconcerned about the consequences for privacy (Honess and Charman, 1992). Given government desire to fund the expansion of CCTV, general public faith in its efficacy, and local government desire to reinvigorate business and shopping environments (Bannister *et al.* 1998) , it is not so surprising that we now have almost 600 town and city centre schemes in England and Wales.

Of course, CCTV is by no means confined to such public spaces – they are merely its most obvious and visible manifestation. CCTV has long been used in private and quasi-private spaces as well. The changing nature and use of city centre space has led to the growth of what has been called 'mass private property': shopping malls, leisure centres, gated communities, and other large complexes (universities, hospitals) which are essentially private property but to which the public (or sections of it) has routine access.

Those responsible for the management of mass private property have also been keen utilisers of CCTV (Shearing and Stenning 1981), and it has formed, so the argument goes, one of the key social control tools in limiting the 'publicness' of such space, facilitating the exclusion of 'flawed consumers' (Bauman 1998). So widespread has the use of CCTV become that Graham (1998) has suggested it is almost a 'fifth utility'. He argues that 'the most striking thing about the wiring up of Britain with CCTV is how similar the process is to the initial development in 19th century cities of the networked utilities that we now all take for granted – gas, water, electricity and telecommunications' (1998: 107). So convinced are people of the powers of CCTV that proposals to extend its use to housing estates – space where the issue of 'privacy' is, one would expect, more problematic – are now under active consideration by government.

Closed-circuit television has become possibly *the* key technology in contemporary strategies for the management of risk. As Rose (1999: 237) puts it, the aim of these strategies 'is to act pre-emptively upon potentially problematic zones, to structure them in such a way as to reduce the likelihood of undesirable events or conduct occurring, and increase the likelihood of those type of events and activities that are desired'. Such a strategy is, we will argue, clearly visible in the rationale for the Kilburn experiment. It is this to experiment that we turn next.

Notes

1 The second was the Prosecution of Offences Act 1985. The Act removed all police responsibility for bringing cases to court.
2 The authors did not have access to data that would allow them to check this. Indeed, there is relatively little data available generally on police custodial populations. In Chapter 3, however, we present an overview of the custodial population at Kilburn between 1999 and 2000.
3 Sufficient data were not available in two of the original sample of 277 cases.
4 The authors note that 'the cost of having CCTV in all the cells [...] may prove prohibitive' (Leigh *et al.* 1998: 83).
5 European Court of Human Rights Case of *McCann and Others* v. *The United Kingdom* (17/1994/464/545), Strasbourg, 27 September 1995.
6 Though described as an 'evaluation', Devon and Cornwall report (Devon and Cornwall Constabulary 2000) was somewhat superficial in character.

Chapter 2

The Kilburn experiment

The background to the Kilburn experiment

In Chapter 1 we considered, in general terms, the issues arising out of the treatment of suspects in custody. We outlined some of the concerns about self-harm and mistreatment of suspects, and looked at the increasing use of CCTV in public places, and the growing pressure to use such technology within police custody suites. What we want to do here is look more closely at the introduction of the very specific experiment – the use of cameras in every cell in a custody suite – in Kilburn, North London during 1999. We begin by looking at the growing use of CCTV within police stations and then consider how and why the Kilburn experiment was devised. We go on to look at how the idea, radical as it was, was received within the Metropolitan Police Service, how it took the shape it eventually did, and how it was 'sold' both internally and externally.

The use of CCTV in custody suites

In the late 1990s a number of police forces began to experiment with the use of CCTV in custody suites. As we outlined in Chapter 1, the 1999 PCA Report on reducing the risks of deaths in custody recommended that 'CCTV coverage of custody suites should be expanded to include one or two observation cells for particularly vulnerable detainees' (1999: 17).

Generally speaking, the use of cameras in most police force areas, where they have been used at all, has been confined to the charge area and the cell corridors. In response to concerns voiced by the PCA, however, some forces gradually introduced cameras into a small number of cells to enable them to monitor especially vulnerable or 'at risk' prisoners, as we outlined in more detail in Chapter 1. The first continuous video recording system in the Metropolitan Police District was introduced in the custody suite at Islington division in 1996. This was followed by cameras in the custody suites at Brixton, Vauxhall and Streatham in early 1997. Small-scale evaluation of these initiatives found that police officers working at the stations concerned tended to feel that the introduction of cameras had improved professional behaviour, provided additional safeguards for both officers and suspects and reduced the number of complaints against police (Metropolitan Police 1997). At this time a number of forces were either introducing cameras into custody suites, or were actively considering so doing. The situation nationwide by the time of the 1999 PCA report was as shown in Table 2.1.

Controversy at Harlesden

The Metropolitan Police policy was to introduce cameras in the booking areas and cell corridors of all its major custody suites, and to consider introducing CCTV into a small number of cells for 'vulnerable' prisoners, including into Kilburn in 1997. And here policy and practice might have stayed but for one particular tragedy in the London Borough of Brent. In the two years prior to the initial proposal to introduce cameras at Kilburn, two men, Marlon Downes and Olusegua Godwin Abbaffi, died whilst in custody in police stations in Brent (the London borough which covers Kilburn). One is alleged to have committed suicide and the other died from natural causes. Marlon Downes' death in particular fuelled the perception locally that detainees, and black detainees in particular, are at considerable risk when in police custody. As part of the wider pre-planned Metropolitan Police policy, CCTV equipment was installed in the booking areas and cell passages at Kilburn during late 1997 but, at that stage, there was no intention of extending the scheme to include coverage of the cells in the custody suite.

The death of Marlon Downes caused considerable local controversy. He was found hanging in his cell in Harlesden police station on the 23 March 1997. Clearly, we are not in a position to comment on what occurred to Marlon Downes. However, it is important to outline the general details of the case, for his death in police custody was the spur for the introduction of cameras into the cells at Kilburn. It is possible, of course, that had such a system existed at the time many questions raised might conceivably have been answered. Within days of Marlon Downes' death Harlesden was closed as a holding station for those in custody and all detainees from that area were to be held at Kilburn police station.

Table 2.1 The use of CCTV in custody suites in England and Wales 1999

Constabulary	CCTV in custody suites?	CCTV in designated cells?
Avon and Somerset	Some	In planning
Cambridgeshire	Some	No
Cheshire	Some	One cell
City of London	Two stations	No
Cleveland	Three out of four	In planning
Cumbria	Piloted in one station	In planning
Derbyshire	Ten stations	Two cells in each of three stations
Devon and Cornwall	All	Two cells at Exeter
Dorset	All major custody centres	One cell in each centre
Durham	All major custody centres	Under consideration
Dyfed and Powys	Two stations	Recommended
Essex	Some	No
Gloucestershire	Three main custody units	No
Greater Manchester	No	No
Gwent	Newport	Three cells at Newport
Hampshire	All major cell blocks	One cell in most blocks
Hertfordshire	In main custody suite	Four vulnerable/drunk cells
Humberside	Under consideration	Under consideration
Kent	In planning	No
Lancashire	No	No
Lincolnshire	In two stations	No
Merseyside	All	No
Metropolitan Police	Many – all planned	Being piloted
Norfolk	In planning	Under consideration
Northumbria	Under consideration	Under consideration
North Yorkshire	In one station	No
Nottinghamshire	Over half of suites	No
South Wales	In all new cell blocks	In planning
South Yorkshire	In planning	No
Staffordshire	Being piloted	Being piloted (one cell)
Suffolk	In planning	In planning (two cells)
Surrey	Yes	Three cells
Sussex	In two sites	In planning
Thames Valley	In planning	No
Warwickshire	Five custody centres	No
West Mercia	Most	In planning
West Midlands	In new stations	No
West Yorkshire	Bradford	No
Wiltshire	All five custody suites	No

Source: Police Complaints Authority (1999)

Marlon Downes had been arrested on the evening of Friday 21 March and his family were told of his death in the early hours of Sunday morning – the 23rd. A family friend was called to be with them and, upon arriving at their house, was urged by a police officer standing outside to persuade Mrs Downes that she should immediately go to Harlesden to identify Marlon. The family needed time to absorb what had happened and, when they felt able to take the next step of identifying Marlon, the police could not say precisely where he had been taken. The first two hospitals the police named were the wrong ones and it was not until mid-morning that the Downes knew that a third, Northwick Park, was the right one to attend. At the hospital they were refused permission to touch Marlon because of the alleged danger of their contaminating evidence that might be present.

Upon arrival at Northwick Park they were met by two officers, as this friend recounted:

> At that time they [police officers] said they'd prepared a statement saying that Marlon had committed suicide and had been found hanging in his cell and committed suicide. We obviously objected at that time because in our view we had no belief at all that that was something that he would have done, that he would have committed suicide. But we also thought it was far too soon, given that they hadn't even carried out an autopsy, and to prepare this statement, without any consultation with the family at all showed a huge amount of insensitivity. But they disregarded that and the statement that they read to us at the time appeared the next day in various papers – that Marlon Downes, 20, found hanging in his cell, committed suicide.
>
> (Interview, June 2000: 3)

The Downes family were eventually able to see the cell in which Marlon died and discovered that the grille from which he had allegedly hanged himself was some ten feet above the bench on which he would have been resting. The police were later to reconstruct events and concluded that he had rolled up two mattresses and stood upon them in order to be able to reach the grille.

Public reaction was immediate and there were calls for an independent public inquiry. The Marlon Downes Memorial Trust was launched, with the objectives of seeking the truth about the circumstances of his death; promoting initiatives to explore the increasing phenomenon of black deaths in custody and raise the profile of deaths in custody; and providing information for the local community regarding civil rights when in contact/conflict with the police.[1]

It was not until the inquest in February 1998 that the family learned all the details of the police evidence. (Coroners are not obliged to reveal evidence prior to the inquest.) Many of the points raised then are directly relevant to this research, in that cell cameras – beyond providing a means of monitoring and potentially keeping detainees safe – are also expected to provide evidence of what happens within cells. For those reasons, we shall enumerate the points at issue during the inquest into the death of Marlon Downes, as follows:

- photos taken in the cell at the time of Marlon Downes' death only showed one mattress;

- expert evidence from a forensic scientist showed that the shoelace with which Marlon Downes had allegedly hanged himself could not support a moving weight of more than nine stone – and he was at least ten stone;

- the written record, showing that Marlon Downes had been physically checked hourly, stated that he had been seen and was alive at least an hour after he had died;

- attempts had been made to erase from the written record an even later check, again confirming he was alive and well, at a time when he was already dead;

- Marlon Downes' solicitor clearly remembered that Marlon was in a particular cell each time he consulted with him, yet Marlon was found in another cell. The police denied he was moved and suggested that the solicitor had been confused;

- the station cleaner was able to clean the cell in which Marlon Downes was found and allegedly detained in, yet cells are not normally cleaned when occupied.

A coroner's inquest is inquisitorial and not adversarial. Rule 36 of the Coroners' Rules of 1984 states:

1   The inquest shall solely determine who the deceased was, how, when and where he came by his death and the particulars required to register the death.

2   Neither the coroner nor the jury shall express any opinion on any other matter.

Following on from this, rule 42 states that no verdict is to appear to determine: (a) criminal liability on the part of a named person; or (b) civil liability. The principle of a fact-finding inquiry without establishing blame is reinforced by rule 22 which states that no witness has to answer questions that may incriminate himself (s.22(1)); and that the coroner should advise (or caution) the witness not to answer such questions (s.22(2) (cited in Whittington 1998: 87). In the case of an unlawful death or a suicide, the criminal standard of proof – beyond all reasonable doubt – must be used.

The inquest into the death of Marlon Downes returned an 'open' verdict, which indicated that the jury could not determine if he had committed suicide or, indeed, if death had been at his own hand. During the inquest a very large number of officers had given evidence corroborating their colleagues' testimonies and the Downes family were left

> in limbo ... it doesn't actually mean anything, open verdict. What it simply means is they couldn't refute one way or the other what had actually happened and given that the whole procedure is about finding the results of someone's death, and establishing how that person died, an open verdict doesn't actually tell you that.
>
> (Interview, June 2000: 6)

Attempting to introduce CCTV in Kilburn

As we have noted, the cells at Harlesden police station were closed almost immediately following Marlon Downes' death. The custody suite at Harlesden was not reopened, partly because of the symbolic effect of keeping it closed, and partly because, having been inspected, though the cells were serviceable, they would have required considerable investment to bring them up to current standards. With the cells closed at Harlesden, and prisoners being kept elsewhere, it was Kilburn that became the site for the CCTV experiment. According to the Borough Commander at the time, 'the beginning quite definitely is with the death of Marlon Downes in the cells at Harlesden'. There were, he said, a number of factors making this a particularly sensitive case for the Metropolitan Police:

> Firstly, the difficulty of seeing how Marlon had met his death in the cell. That's to all concerned ... [everyone] was bemused as to how this could have taken place because it wasn't immediately

obvious...Secondly, was the fact that this was a black man, in Harlesden which although it's a relatively peaceful community...there is a suspicion of the police...and this was to prove no exception to that. This was to prove a trigger to the anti-police sentiment that was around, understandably so...Thus, while any death in custody is tragic, this one had particular circumstances which required a lot of hard work to understand, to explain to people.

(Interview, March 2001)

An investigation commenced immediately, under the supervision of the PCA. This, predictably, was a particularly difficult period. The Downes family had a lot of questions about how Marlon's death had occurred, questions which, at that stage, could not be answered. The absence of clear information undoubtedly fuelled local suspicions and concerns. As the Borough Commander put it, 'that delay was to provide a great deal of fear and apprehension within the community, that allowed the rumour mill to get going'. At this stage a public campaign started, and there were demonstrations outside the police station, public meetings and the beginnings of what was to become in time a more substantial campaign.

It was against this background that the Borough Commander and others began to look for ways of altering the custody suite and/or the ways in which it was managed and run. There were a number of problems to be faced, he suggested:

I had a number of circumstances that were unsatisfactory from my point of view. One, as a police officer I could not provide the evidence as to how someone had met their death. The best we had was well-founded theory. But as to evidence, it was evidence of what didn't happen, rather than what did happen...Secondly, I had a duty of care towards my police officers and I couldn't actually say to them that I personally was convinced one way or the other...I had a responsibility to the family, and to the wider community and, again, I couldn't satisfy them, and they were asking pertinent questions that couldn't be readily answered in a way that I would have liked to have done. So those were all the immediate factors; thinking 'why are we in this situation'? Is there a way in which we could get round it?...I felt decidedly uncomfortable that I couldn't provide hard and fast answers that I felt a number of different elements deserved.

(Interview, March 2001)

Within a very short time, the idea of using CCTV had emerged. In fact, the initial idea arose in conversation between the Borough Commander and Paul Boateng, the constituency MP. Both the Borough Commander and Paul Boateng were apparently generally convinced that introducing CCTV was the right way forward.

The idea of using CCTV in the reception areas of custody suites was reasonably well established at this time and was beginning to be rolled out throughout the Metropolitan Police District. However, as we have suggested, the use of cameras in cells remained unusual. The idea was taken up with some enthusiasm by the Brent Borough Commander, who saw CCTV in the cells as one means by which the Metropolitan Police might begin to rebuild community confidence in the treatment of suspects in custody. The idea was innovative in that it was a case of using '...old technology [to] resolve these issues, and not only for this particular case, but really for any other allegation about the handling of prisoners while they are in custody'. It was not, however, an idea that took hold quickly. The Metropolitan Police initially investigated whether it was feasible, practically, to put cameras in all the cells within a custody suite, and what the likely financial cost would be. Having done so, there was also the question of public consultation as well as getting the approval of the Metropolitan Police generally.

Consultation was undertaken with the local courts, with defence lawyers and others using the custody suite. Indeed, linked with this, we were invited in to discuss the possibility of an independent evaluation, part of which was to involve interviews with detainees prior to the cameras going in. According to the Borough Commander, 'some of the early findings from that [were used] to check that people weren't going to be completely fazed by the idea of cameras going in the cells'. The idea of installing cameras in the cells was put to the local Police Community Consultative Group. The PCCG backed the idea and 'wrote to the Commissioner and the Home Office with that decision, that we agreed with CCTV going in the cells'.[2] Contact was also maintained, according to the police, with the Marlon Downes Trust who were supportive of the idea of introducing CCTV. According to the Borough Commander:

> I think that some of those involved in the Trust perceived that we were acting genuinely, and although we couldn't bring Marlon Downes back, at least some good might come from his death. I think they were content for [the CCTV experiment] to proceed.

A briefing paper was produced in December 1998 by the staff officer to the Borough Commander in Brent outlining the possible installation of

CCTV in custody cells in Kilburn. The paper noted the local background factors, notably the two deaths in custody, and more generally 'a perception [that] has developed in some sections of the local black community that the police are deliberately mistreating certain types of detainees'. The Metropolitan Police (MPS), as were many others forces, was already in the midst of a programme of modernising its custody suites. This programme included designing safer cells (removing potential ligature points); encouraging greater use of the FME (Forensic Medical Examiner) service; and the proposed introduction of a new custody officer course, with particular emphasis on the care of prisoners and the identification of vulnerable prisoners. In addition, in early 1998 the MPS took a decision to introduce CCTV cameras into the booking areas of its main suites and to consider introducing cameras into selected cells. As part of this modernisation programme CCTV was introduced in Kilburn, though it was confined at that time to the charging areas and cell passages.

The Borough Commander in particular was concerned that this did not go far enough and strongly encouraged a much more radical experiment with CCTV. The proposal was for cameras to be put in every cell in the custody suite 'in an effort to restore confidence at a local level regarding the treatment of prisoners at [Kilburn police] station'. According to the briefing paper, this proposal was said to have the backing of local MPs Paul Boateng (by then a Home Office Minister) and Ken Livingstone, and of Debbie Nimblette, the head of the Marlon Downes' Memorial Trust.

The objectives of the proposed experiment at that stage were:

- to secure the funding and installation of CCTV equipment in the custody cells at Kilburn;

- to identify the strengths and weaknesses regarding the practical use of the equipment;

- to evaluate the opportunities and threats regarding:
  – greater public reassurance;
  – the legal issues and human rights considerations;
  – the ability to rebut allegations in civil claims;
  – the impact of such equipment on the assessment of prisoners suffering from mental illness;
  – the ability to prevent criminal damage to police property, bringing criminal charges where appropriate;
  – the day-to-day implications of operating such a system.

The existing cameras in the charge area and corridors had been installed by a firm called ClearView Communications Ltd as part of their ongoing contract with the MPS for the installation of CCTV in all custody suites. At the time the proposal for a further experiment was made the company indicated that it would be willing to supply seventeen cameras, installing one in each cell and detention room, together with suitable recording equipment to provide 24-hour recording. The expected cost was in the region of £30,000. ClearView were themselves willing to underwrite a significant part of the costs, largely because of the profile of the experiment. The force locally then started to explore other avenues for the rest of the funding, including the possibility of sponsorship – which they were told was unlikely to be forthcoming – and support from the Area HQ[3] and the Operational and Technical Support Unit in the MPS's Department of Technology. At the same time, attention was also turned to the question of the possibility of external evaluation, as well as to considering the legal issues, particularly concerning the areas of privacy and human rights.

The constraints, assumptions and risks related to the proposed project were also considered:[4]

Constraints
- this project would take place before any business case had assessed wider installation throughout the MPS.

Assumptions
- that installation would not contravene current human rights obligations or legislation;
- that the evaluation process would include the external contributors identified (Goldsmiths College);
- that the Operational Use of Video Steering Group (OUVSG) would need to be consulted during the process.

Risks
- the pilot would be contrary to current MPS policy;
- it would infringe civil liberties when tested in the courts;
- it would erode public confidence in the police;
- it would not prevent unwanted occurrences, e.g. self-harm incidents.

This briefing paper also made clear that 'the cameras were to be overt and clear signs would indicate that they were in operation'. Also, that it was 'accepted that the toilet area [would] probably remain out of view in the interests of privacy'.

As was mentioned above, one of the anticipated areas of consultation was with the Operational Use of Video Steering Group. This committee, which met at New Scotland Yard approximately every two months, was set up to consider policy and practice in relation to CCTV monitoring by the MPS. It had been dormant for some time, but was resurrected as a means both of ensuring that there was general force policy over the use of CCTV and regulating the nature and extent of local 'experiments'. At the time the experiment was being proposed it was chaired by a superintendent or detective superintendent, though formally it reported to an assistant commissioner. The committee contained representatives from numerous Metropolitan Police operational departments as well as the Police Federation and the Solicitors' Branch. Its remit covered public CCTV as well as its use in other spaces, such as police stations. The proposed Kilburn experiment was first outlined to OUVSG at their meeting in February 1999. Authority to proceed was held in abeyance until legal opinion had been received.

The Borough Commander, in seeking legal opinion, outlined what he took to be the importance of the proposed experiment. He said:

> This initiative is a real opportunity to pilot a confidence-building approach to detention in an area where relations between parts of the community and police are at a low ebb, with many allegations and more accusations of ill-treatment whilst in police custody. It has the active support of Paul Boateng and is supported by the Brent [Police] Consultative Group.
>
> (Memo from Chief Superintendent Paul Green
> to Metropolitan Police solicitors, 19 December 1998)

Initial legal opinion from the Metropolitan Police solicitor to the Borough Commander raised a number of potential problems with the proposed scheme. The legal opinion noted the PCA guidance that 'at least one cell should be covered by CCTV so that those known to be particularly at risk can be kept under constant observation', and pointed out that it would be incumbent on the Metropolitan Police to explain why it was necessary and proper to 'go over and beyond' such guidance. In particular, the solicitor raised the following queries:

- [What would the response be] to questioning on the ethos behind paragraph 12.2 of Code C [of the PACE *Codes of Practice*] whereby in any period of 24 hours a detained person must be allowed a continuous period of at least eight hours for rest, free from questioning, travel or any interruption by police officers in connection with the investigation concerned? Does that not imply a general rule to let a detained person rest on their own in privacy and without anything to disturb that rest, such as constant observation on CCTV?

- Could a detained person argue that to be constantly under scrutiny amounted to oppression such as would affect the admissibility of any admissions/confession on interview?

- Could there be a problem under Article 3 of the Convention [on Human Rights] which states that no one shall be subjected to degrading treatment?

(Solicitor's advice (CO 6), 15 January 1999)

The response of New Scotland Yard to the Solicitor's advice was to encourage further exploration of the proposed experiment at Kilburn, though noting that 'the critical issue appears to be the number of cells that should be equipped with CCTV'.[5] One or two cells could be fully justified 'when a prisoner is deemed to be either a deliberate self risk or in need of extra monitoring', but 'equipping all cells would be hard to justify in accordance with Human Rights legislation'.

There were numerous subsequent meetings involving officers from the borough, and representatives of various departments at New Scotland Yard to discuss whether, and in what form, the Kilburn pilot might go ahead. Further legal advice was sought from the force solicitor. In seeking legal opinion the following questions were asked:

- would the installation of cameras into all the cells and detention rooms be lawful?

- would civil liberties be infringed unlawfully by using such cameras?

- are there legal constraints concerning viewing of monitors and tapes or regarding the provision of 24-hour recording?

- are there any other issues or implications which would adversely affect the viability of this project?

(Request for legal opinion and advice, Inspector Shaylor, undated)

Legal opinion, provided to OUVSG at their meeting in June 1999, was also unsupportive. The Metropolitan Police solicitor expressed the view that the system as proposed (cameras in all cells with continuous 24-hour monitoring) would raise problems relating to privacy. She went further and said that an alternative proposal for a 'closed system' (cameras in all cells with 24-recording, but only post-hoc viewing) was also open to criticism on similar grounds. Her conclusion was that an 'open system' (24-hour continuous monitoring), only in cells suitable for vulnerable prisoners, was the most acceptable way forward. It was agreed at the meeting that a decision regarding the Kilburn experiment would be further delayed while more inquiries were made and, more particularly, whilst visits were made to other forces to inspect their custody suite CCTV operations.[6]

Visits were made to police stations in Bournemouth and Newport prior to the July 1999 meeting of the OUSVG.[7] Initially, there had been only one cell in Newport covered by CCTV. From July 1998 this had been extended to three cells within the custody suite. There are no toilets in these cells and detainees are advised to ask custody staff to take them to an appropriate toilet. At the time there was no protocol covering the identification of vulnerable prisoners to be placed in the cells covered by CCTV. On the basis of brief discussions with those responsible for the system, there did appear to be clear support for the CCTV scheme from both custody staff and the Chief Constable. They had no plans for extending the scheme to a greater number of cells.

CCTV cameras were installed in one 'drunk cell' in Bournemouth's custody suite in early 1999. Also installed by ClearView, the camera covering the cell records in colour, requiring there to be a low-level light on at all times. The camera in the cell views the toilet area and detainees are advised that if they do not want to be filmed they can ask staff to take them to a private toilet. Again, there appeared to be clear support from custody staff and, according to the police, there was also support among lay visitors and local solicitors.

In the period following these visits, and after the subsequent meeting of OUSVG, there was considerable debate and argument about how Kilburn should proceed, if at all. There were several points at which it appeared that the introduction of in-cell CCTV would not go ahead at all in Kilburn. As already suggested, there was concern at New Scotland Yard about two aspects of the Kilburn proposal; firstly, that it would cover all cells and, secondly, that it would involve continuous surveillance. There was strong pressure to reduce the scope of the Kilburn experiment, either by limiting the number of cells that would contain cameras or by limiting the use of the recordings to retrospective viewing only. The latter was referred to as a 'closed' system. An 'open' system involving continuous viewing was considered to be 'high risk'. In the event a proposal by an officer, acting on behalf of the Deputy Assistant Commissioner in charge of considering the Kilburn application, came down in favour of an 'open system', but restricted to a limited number of cells. In his submission to the OUSVG the officer said that 'an open system would allow custody staff to observe, via a monitor, vulnerable prisoners in a designated "safety" cell'. Senior officers at Kilburn, however, were quite against restricting the use of cameras to a limited number of cells for 'vulnerable' prisoners. The Borough Commander explained his objections in the following way:

> I was keen to keep full CCTV coverage. There were other sites, Cardiff I think was one, that had partial CCTV coverage. The implication being that you identify the person at risk and put them in a cell for monitoring. As you would do if you had an open door of a cell if you felt that someone was at risk of suicide. That to me just exacerbated the worst features, because you can't always tell. Nobody anticipated that Marlon would take his own life. He was not identified as a suicide risk at all. No history of making attempts, seen by external people who had no indication whatsoever that he was likely to make an attempt on his life. That man would not have been put into a CCTV-covered cell. No reason to. Of course, you then have a suspicion when someone like that commits suicide – 'why wasn't he put in the cell? It was because you were going to do something to him'. So by introducing an element of choice into it you actually make it more difficult for the custody officer, you create suspicion if things do go wrong, quite needlessly. The cost difference between cameras in two cells and cameras in all the cells is also marginal.

In response to the Yard's presentation of their position to OUVSG, the Chief Inspector at Kilburn, responsible at that stage for leading on the proposed experiment, outlined the local division's position. They too, he said, rejected the idea of a 'closed' system as failing to provide the protection they desired. However, whilst in broad agreement with the stated MPS policy (outlined above), Kilburn still wished to depart from this and to install cameras in all the cells in the police station. This was to be a 'pilot' he suggested, subject to independent evaluation. In his view the gains and risks were as follows:

Gains
- police 'duty of care' can be extended to all detainees within the cells through observation;
- provides an audit trail of all detainees' movements within police custody, thus improving community perception of all suspects' treatment by police;
- removes from the custody officer the 'decision-making process' about who to place in identified 'safety' cell;
- those prisoners not immediately identified as 'vulnerable' through the proposed protocol could still be monitored for signs of risk/self-harm;
- better defence of complaints/civil actions by monitoring the complete custody area.

Associated risks/concerns
- concerns under Article 8 Human Rights Act (right to privacy) as identified by Metropolitan Police solicitor;
- concerns about staff availability to monitor seventeen separate cameras on a multiplex screen;
- subsequent liability of custody staff should an incident be recorded where appropriate action is not taken due to other duties taking precedence at the time;
- the future roll-out of a system covering all the cells would have implications for initial costings and later servicing/repair of equipment that are greater than the proposed MPS model;
- the volume of visual information may be overwhelming;
- coverage of toilet area would cause concern when detainee was not identified as vulnerable.

As we have already suggested, there were times when it appeared that the experiment might not proceed. The Borough Commander was confident, however, that he would be able to secure support from Scotland Yard:

> I didn't really have any doubt that it would take place because of the political will behind it. That was always the trump card I had in my back pocket. Put in the context of where [the Metropolitan Police was] in terms of the Lawrence Inquiry, in terms of concerns

about minority communities, the fact that you have more black people than white people dying in the cells. This wasn't state of the art technology. This was something that if seen to work could be incorporated into future design processes.

After further discussion within Scotland Yard the go-ahead was given for the full 'pilot' at Kilburn and preparations were made for the installation of cameras.

Placing the cameras

The cell cameras were installed during a week in mid-January 2000, while detainees were temporarily held at Harrow Road police station. The final cost was approximately £48,000. All fifteen cells had a camera placed in a corner, at ceiling level, which directly faced the toilet and observed all movement within the cell. No area was excluded from the gaze of the camera and initial thoughts of electronically masking the toilet area, to provide privacy, were dismissed. This was largely because of fears that detainees might use the toilets to dispose of evidence. The two detention rooms used for juveniles are of a different design and two cameras were required in each to cover the entire area. Unlike the cameras used in the custody area, the cell cameras had no audio link. The opportunity provided by an empty custody suite facilitated the redesign of both the custody and bailed-to-return desks, both of which had previously left officers feeling unsafe during their dealings with detainees. The very cramped conditions within the suite did not allow much scope for improvement, but the booking desk was raised from the floor and reinforced with a clear plexiglas shield to provide some immediate protection from possible assault. Space did not permit the same treatment for the bailed-to-return desk.

How do the cameras work?

On 26 January 2000, as detainees were again taken to Kilburn, the cameras were first used. Two new monitors had been placed on the booking desk, between and facing the custody sergeants. The cameras filmed each cell in its entirety and focused directly upon the toilet. One monitor could show sixteen cells at once, but in practice it was generally used to focus on just four at a time, as the picture was more distinct. Used in this way, the image moved from cell to cell, with an approximate four second exposure time for each. It was also possible to have that monitor focus solely on one cell, should officers not wish to view what was happening in another cell when the monitor was in multiple-image mode. The other, smaller monitor was focused on one selected cell and was intended to be used for the close observation of those thought to be at risk or vulnerable in particular ways. The smaller monitor could also view each cell consecutively. Officers working at the desk were themselves watched by a camera, to ensure that the monitors were not improperly observed, such as when strip searches were taking place.

The custody suite is now almost completely under the surveillance of the cameras, with the only exceptions being the FME's room, the consultation and interview rooms, the property room and the evidential breath machine room.

The video recording equipment is in a small room which itself is subject to video surveillance. The machine already in use for recording the rest of the custody suite was augmented to provide additional coverage and now contains six VCRs; three for the cells and detention rooms and three for the communal areas. The tapes used are four hours long but actually run for eight hours, because they are run on a time-lapse system. In practice this means that every two seconds of real time are recorded on one second of tape time.

At Kilburn gaolers are responsible for changing the tapes (or custody sergeants, when a gaoler is unavailable). Tapes have to be changed three times a day and they are timed to coincide with the start of the three shifts, beginning at midnight, 8 a.m. and 4 p.m. The system is designed so that there will always be six tapes in the machine; two recording and four as back-up. As each one is completed another is inserted so that there is always a margin for error. Gaolers are alerted by a warning bleep, which becomes a continuous warning tone should the tape be finished.

Upon removal from the machine the tape's edge is labelled as being from the CCTV together with the shift code, day and date. This information is duplicated on the top face of the tape and is augmented by an exhibit reference number corresponding to one already reserved in the exhibit book. The tape is then placed in its cardboard sleeve and sealed by a video tape seal which has been signed by the gaoler. Tape details are entered into the exhibit book and the processed tape is placed in the property cupboard for collection the following day by property store staff. The tape is then further documented prior to storage. At Kilburn the property cupboard is in a room that lacks a camera and is frequently opened for other purposes each day. All tapes are finally stored in metal filing cabinets in a room some distance from the custody suite. The room is not temperature controlled and, in summer, can be very hot. There are therefore some concerns about whether tapes might deteriorate if they are kept for any length of time.

Into the unknown

The pilot scheme was officially launched in the custody suite on 14 March 2000. At the official launch of the scheme, the local Borough Commander said:

> three years ago there was a death of a person in custody. After all the inquiries had taken place and the inquest held, it was clear the police had one view of what happened and the family another. With the CCTV system we can monitor people in cells and provide a record of their time in there.
>
> (*Evening Standard*, 14 March 2000)

The theme of local perceptions of the police was picked up by the Deputy Assistant Commissioner present who said, 'the CCTV scheme will allow for complete transparency of police treatment of prisoners, enhance prisoner care and improve community confidence in Brent Police, (*The Job*, 24 March 2000). Mrs Downes was herself informed about the opening, just prior to its happening, by a local journalist who wanted her to comment on the scheme. She eventually agreed to attend the launch, because she wished to honour the memory of her son, but this perceived failure to keep the Trust informed was, she felt, not unusual. There remains considerable scepticism in parts of the local community about the Metropolitan Police's motives in installing the cameras at Kilburn, and a continuing feeling among some members of the Trust that they have been used by the police as a means of legitimising already existing plans. Whatever the reality, what this illustrates is the considerable distance there is to go before better relations of trust are established between the Metropolitan Police and parts of the local communities it serves.

The untimely death of Marlon Downes forms both the backdrop to this research and, in many ways, raises some of the major questions and issues that were its focus. In the chapters that follow we explore how the CCTV experiment at Kilburn worked in practice, how it was experienced by those held in custody in police cells, and consider the extent to which some of the answers might have been available had CCTV been installed in the cells on the morning of 23 March 1997.

Notes

1 *Willesden and Brent Chronicle*, 19 June 1997.
2 Interview Three, November 2000.
3 At this time the Metropolitan Police was divided into six areas. Kilburn fell within what was then referred to as No. 2 area.
4 *Installation of CCTV in custody cells at Kilburn Operational Command Unit*. Briefing paper. December 1998.
5 Memo from CO 30 to Chief Supt Green, 25 January 1999.
6 Operational Use of Video Steering Group, Minutes of the meeting of 1 June 1999.
7 Researchers from Goldsmiths accompanied MPS staff on these visits.

Chapter 3

The custody suite: who are the detainees?

Venturing into the custody suite of any police station, it is generally impossible to predict what awaits. At times they can be unnervingly busy and fraught places.

Take a Monday morning – similar to one witnessed in the study – when it is likely, after a hectic weekend and no court sittings, that most of the cells will be occupied. There is a van waiting in the yard to take detainees to court, with private security staff milling around the booking desk, anxious to be away and on the road. Officers are having to complete the appropriate paperwork and ensure that property has been restored before detainees can be released. One of the detainees is anxious and agitated, but the procedures have to be carried out correctly and cannot be rushed. At the same time another officer is booking in a new prisoner, while others are held in a queue, awaiting their turn. The station is close to Willesden, where Eurostar trains are cleaned, and a non-English speaking asylum seeker has decamped from the train and been arrested. He will need an interpreter, but there is a shortage, so nothing can be done with him until one is free to come to the station; in the meanwhile, he has to be placed in a cell. The gaoler responds to a cell buzzer and also has to carry out the cell checks. She has been ferrying breakfast to the various cells and, unsurprisingly, detainees want to be allowed to wash before they are taken to court. The cells do not contain basins, so another officer remains with each detainee as they take it in turns to use the basin in the cell corridor.

Gradually, some of the cells are cleared while others continue to hold those awaiting interview. The pace slackens a little – and then another arrestee arrives.

Take another day, perhaps early evening, mid-week. There is one detainee in the cells, drunk and asleep, and he needs to be checked and roused every quarter of an hour. The officers have no one else to care for. They sit behind their desk, waiting for something to happen. Something inevitably will, but they have no way of knowing when. For the custody staff, work in the custody suite has no predictable pattern beyond the incessant filling out of forms and checking of cells. Familiar faces will appear before them, but there is also an endless flow of new ones, each with their own anxieties and fears, which are sometimes masked by aggression and fuelled by alcohol or drugs.

Throughout this book we will talk about 'detainees': prisoners in police custody for varying lengths of time. Who are these people who inhabit the cells? What are their backgrounds? Are they old? Young? Mostly male? In this chapter we look in detail at the client group passing through Kilburn police station. In doing so we provide a unique snapshot of a year and a half in the life of a police station.

We amassed a considerable amount of data from the police records, all of it made more interesting because of the relative rarity of such an exercise. Beyond describing the flow of people through the custody suite, our primary concern is to identify the nature and size of particular groups that may have special needs or qualities requiring special attention or consideration. There is then the question of whether the installation of CCTV in the cells appeared to have any discernible impact on the operation of the custody suite.[1]

Understanding the records

Each police force has its own custody record form. The forms used by the Metropolitan Police begin with a set of fairly standard questions about the detainee. The first page and a half of the custody record, Form 57, is computer-generated and records personal details of the detainee; reason(s) for arrest; reason(s) for detention; whether legal advice has been requested or declined; whether or not an appropriate adult or an interpreter has been used; and whether or not a consulate or embassy has been informed about the detainee. Not all of this section of the record will necessarily be complete. Should a detainee be impaired through drink or drugs, or needing the help of an appropriate adult, they might be unable to indicate whether or not they require legal advice, or give their place of birth and age. Some detainees refuse to give any details at all, or deliberately give incorrect details.

The remainder of Form 57 is handwritten, with each entry being individually signed by the recording officer. It should give complete details of every action involving the detainee: how often they are checked in the cell; allowed to use the telephone; visited by the FME (Forensic Medical Examiner, or doctor); taken to the consultation room; provided with a meal and so forth. *Nothing* involving the detainee should be omitted from the written record.

The custody record also contains a continuation sheet, Form 57M, relating to the need for an appropriate adult and/or medical care. This is of particular importance because its accurate completion determines the level of support offered to detainees, who are asked if they have reading problems; learning difficulties or disabilities; attended a special school; a mental health problem or suffer from a mental illness. An affirmative to any of these generally means that an appropriate adult will be required. Anyone 16 and under must, by law, be seen and assisted by an appropriate adult. The final section on medical needs provides information about the detainee's general state of health and also asks specifically about whether they have ever attempted self-harm.

Other papers found in each file might include the FME's report(s), copies of warrants and immigration papers. A property record is routinely included. Potentially, there is a great deal of paperwork to be completed by the police and much of this centres on the handwritten records compiled by the custody officer or gaoler. More officers will be contributing to the record as each new shift takes over and the longer the detainee is in custody. When the custody suite is particularly busy an officer might not write each entry at precisely the time listed, and some entries are entered retrospectively but not listed as such. Occasionally officers will fail to enter the time the detainee's custody ends. Officers will sometimes write very full notes explaining an action taken, perhaps signalling that the decision needed extra justification. The accuracy of the records is further dependent upon the assisting gaoler(s) providing precise information and carrying out effective checks. There are times when the gaolers' inexperience means they need a greater degree of supervision than busy periods might necessarily permit. Overall, the final responsibility for each detainee rests with the custody officer.

Some of the information on which this chapter is based could, theoretically, have been derived directly from the police computerised records, had this been permitted. The handwritten element – often the largest part of each record – and the fact that some data are incorrectly entered precluded this.

Examining the records

We examined 7,962 records, beginning with those for May 1999 and ending with those for September 2000. Each record had a corresponding number but, sometimes, there was no record attached to that number. The police could not simply reuse a number which they had 'opened in error'; they had to insert that particular record in the master file so that there was evidence of what had happened at a given time. This means that the number of records we *appear* to have examined does not tally with the actual number available for inspection, so for a very small proportion of records there are no attached data. Within each master file of records there were also usually some missing. Quite often officers would have removed them because they were dealing with detainees who had been bailed to return and individuals' records needed to be updated. The percentage of missing or 'opened in error' records was approximately 4 per cent. Each available record was read and data extracted. Because of the reasons given earlier not all records were complete. In most cases, therefore, the final figures are some way below the maximum of 7,962.

A note on ethnicity

Form 57 requires that the police enter details of ethnic origin based on six groupings: White European; dark-skinned European (commonly entered as Mediterranean); Afro-Caribbean (AC); Asian; Oriental; Arabic. For this research we also identified anyone born in either Ulster or Eire, because of their large representation in the local community. We have shown the Irish as one group, as it was not always possible to determine whether some of these detainees had been born in the North or South because officers would simply put 'Ireland' when entering their place of birth. We did not attempt to identify other individual ethnic groups living within the research area.

All ethnic categorisations are based on police observation, rather than on detainees' self-identification. A British-born detainee could be labelled as any of the above, depending upon their appearance and their place of birth (when given). All detainees perceived to be black (rather than Asian, Arabic or Oriental) are entered as 'AC' irrespective of whether they are, for example, Afro-Caribbean, Black African or Black Other. The term White European is used by the police to describe most apparently-white British-born detainees, but may also be used by the police to refer to someone born, for example, in Canada, France or Australia. Some distinct ethnic groups might be ascribed various identities: one Kosovan might be described as Mediterranean, whilst another Kosovan could be described as White European by the same custody officer. The fundamental point, therefore, is that the data on the ethnicity of detainees cannot be treated as an accurate reflection of how detainees would categorise themselves. What can be relied upon is that the data reflect police perceptions of the ethnicity of detainees. This, in itself, is very important for, arguably, it is precisely these perceptions that influence police treatment of detainees.

Who were the detainees?

Age

Male detainees comprised just over 90 per cent of the sample and females almost 10 per cent. Nearly 50 per cent were under 27 years of age and a third were 21 years of age or less. During the course of the study, the youngest person held in custody was 10 years old and the oldest was 82.

Table 3. 1 Age of male and female detainees (%)

Age	Males	Females	Total
16 and under	10	11	10
17–21	23	17	23
22–30	30	28	29
31–40	25	31	26
41–50	8	9	8
50+	4	4	4
Total	100	100	100

Table 3.1 shows that the vast majority of detainees (88 per cent) were aged under 40. One-tenth of all those held in custody were juveniles and approximately one-third of detainees are aged 21 or younger. The ages of male and female detainees are roughly similar.

Ethnicity

As can be seen from Table 3.2, those detained and identified by the police as being White European, and additionally by us as being Irish,[2] comprised 45 per cent of the total. The remaining 55 per cent were, in police terms, non-white. This is very close to the general demography of the local area which, according to police data, has a non-white population of 54 per cent. A slightly higher proportion of female than male detainees was White.

Table 3.2 Ethnicity of male and female detainees (%)

Ethnicity	Males	Females	Total
White European	33	43	34
Irish	11	9	11
Afro-Caribbean	42	38	41
Asian	7	3	6
Mediterranean	5	4	5
Oriental	–	2	1
Arabic	2	1	2
	100	100	100

From police records it was possible to ascertain that 32 per cent of detainees were not born in the United Kingdom or Eire. However, it was impossible to identify the percentage who were actually foreign nationals. (Section 12 of Form 57, relating to foreign nationals, was rarely completed and very few detainees asked that their embassy be informed of their arrest.) While 57 per cent of detainees were born in the United Kingdom, actual place of birth was no indicator of citizenship; a detainee born in Bangladesh, New Zealand or Jamaica may well have been a British citizen, permanently resident in the United Kingdom. The overall picture, however, is one of ethnic diversity. Kilburn police station is based in a multicultural community within a vast city through which a very broad range of people passes. This diversity is clearly visible within the custody suite.

Reasons for arrest

We have grouped reasons for arrest in broad general categories. Table 3.3 shows the major categories of offences leading to arrest (in some cases more than one main charge was recorded and this is included within the figures in the table). Not noted in this table are the 3 per cent of illegal immigrants, asylum seekers and over-stayers facing deportation. They are significant because of the sometimes disproportionate amount of time they spend in police cells while awaiting deportation or removal to an immigration detention centre. Slightly over 2 per cent of sexual offences are also omitted from this table.

Table 3.3 Main reasons for arrest (%)

Reasons for arrest	Males	Females
Public order	22	27
Theft/handling	16	16
Criminal damage	6	7
Drugs	12	6
Violence	12	11
Motoring	9	6

Note: percentages do not total 100

What is not shown here is that a higher proportion of women were arrested for fraud than were men (6 per cent, versus 2 per cent). A higher proportion of women were also detained as illegal immigrants (6 per cent, versus 3 per cent of men). It must be remembered, however, that women comprised only 10 per cent of all detainees arrested and held at the station.

If we look more closely at reasons for arrest some differences among different ethnic groups are visible. These differences become particularly important when we come on to discuss those who are subjected to strip searches, as the nature of the offence is one of the factors influencing a decision to conduct such a search. Table 3.4 looks at the ethnic origin of detainees divided into the major arrest categories.

Table 3.4 Reasons for arrest by ethnic origin of detainees (%)

Reasons for arrest	White European	Irish	Afro-Caribbean	Asian	Total
Public order	29	35	14	22	22
Theft/handling	14	14	17	17	16
Criminal damage	7	6	5	6	6
Drugs	9	4	16	14	12
Violence	12	12	11	15	12
Motoring	9	11	7	11	9

Note: percentages do not total 100

Length of stay in cells

Just over two-fifths of detainees were held at the station for no more than four hours and approximately three-fifths were detained for six hours or less. Of those arrested and taken to the station, just over one-fifth (23 per cent) were held overnight and overall 3 per cent were held for more than 36 hours. There were no major differences between male and female detainees in length of time detained.

It was impossible to gain an entirely accurate picture of how frequently cells were checked. It was easier to determine those who received both quarter- and half-hour checks (2 per cent and 22 per cent, respectively) because these figures were more consistently entered in the record. Only a third could be positively identified as being on hourly checks. Over two-fifths (44 per cent) could not be classified at all. One of the reasons for this was undoubtedly linked to the length of time individual detainees spent at the station and another was the frequency of their consultations with solicitors, and interviews with officers. Apart from the foregoing reasons, it is impossible for us to say why such a large number of detainees were not checked consistently; at times it seemed, from comparing consecutive records, that if a detainee's check were missed, for whatever reason, then that detainee's next check would be delayed until all the cells were being inspected. The major imperative seemed to be to have uniform checks, rather than to be checking detainees individually at the time actually required.

The great majority of detainees – 83 per cent – were released back into the community, though almost a third (32 per cent) were bailed to return to the station for final decisions to be made regarding charges. Thirteen per cent were taken straight to court and the remaining 4 per cent were either returned to prison, deported, sent to secure accommodation under the Mental Health Act or sent to hospital. Again, when comparisons were made by gender, there were few differences apart from the fact that proportionately fewer women than men were sent directly to court (10 per cent, versus 13 per cent of males).

Doing time in the station

This brief 'snapshot' of detainees provides a backdrop for the examination we now undertake of what happens to detainees when they are in the station. What are detainees' entitlements? What are the procedures? Whom do they see?

Medical attention

Under the PACE *Codes of Conduct* (C9.4) an FME must be called 'as soon as practicable' should a detainee request one. Of course, Form 57M might have alerted officers to specific details, such as histories of self-harm, but this is dependent upon the accuracy of information provided by detainees. Under the *Codes* (C9.2), officers must call an FME should they be concerned about the physical or mental state of any detainee. This means that officers will sometimes take the 'safe' option of calling an FME to ensure that a detainee is in a fit state to be detained or interviewed. To be 'fit' is to be physically and mentally well and not under the influence of drink or drugs. Officers must have this assurance regarding a detainee's state if they are to proceed with all the formalities of detention. To be certified fit for detention or interview is the primary reason for a detainee's examination by an FME.

Forty-seven per cent of detainees – almost half the sample – were seen by the FME. This is an extraordinarily high figure. Most previous research has noted rates of less than 10 per cent (Brown 1997) and this raises important questions about why the figure should be quite so high at this station. As Table 3.5 shows, there was a range of reasons for calling an FME beyond those already outlined (the table notes the reasons given within the total population seen by an FME).

Table 3.5 Reasons for being seen by FME*

Reason for decision	Percentage
Pre-existing medical condition etc.	32
Receiving treatment for above	26
On medication	22
Had attempted self-harm	7
Injury	20
Needs appropriate adult?	4
Unfit through drink	44
Addicted to drugs	12

Note: multiple reasons may exist and percentages do not total 100%

Over two-fifths of those seen by an FME (approximately one-fifth of all those detained in custody during the period) were deemed to be 'unfit through drink'. One-third of those seen by an FME had a pre-existing medical condition, and illicit drugs were involved in the cases of over one-tenth of those seen.

In addition to the reasons listed in the table nearly 8 per cent of those seen by an FME had mental health problems, 4 per cent were asthmatic, while some had to have body samples taken to measure levels of intoxication.

Looking more closely at those who were seen by an FME we can see a pattern emerging. The possibility of being seen, or needing to be seen, by an FME increased with age. For example, 28 per cent of juveniles saw an FME whereas 58 per cent of those in the 31–40 age bracket saw one. The major exception lay with those suffering – or appearing to suffer – an injury, when this trend was reversed. It was the under-16s and those between the ages of 17 and 21, rather than their older counterparts, who were most likely to be injured. Those with addiction problems were more likely to be between the ages of 22 and 40.

Women were more likely to see an FME than were men. More women than men were on medication and more women had, and were receiving treatment for, a pre-existing injury. Of special note was the fact that, proportionately, over twice as many women as men had attempted self-harm. There were also gender differences in relation to other reasons for seeing an FME, women being more likely to have problems with mental health and asthma. The major exception to all these was the category of 'injury', when women were half as likely as men to need the attention of an FME. As well, fewer women were assessed as being unfit through alcohol.

Receiving legal advice

All detainees are entitled to receive free legal advice during any stage of their detention. (They are also told that they may speak privately to a solicitor by telephone, but that is a physical impossibility at Kilburn.) Forty-five per cent of detainees indicated that they wished to have the services of a solicitor. This did not mean that they all actually saw one; rather, it was an expression of intent which some did not pursue because they were discharged almost immediately from the station, or for some other reason. We did not attempt to ascertain how many asked for, but did not see, a solicitor or accredited legal representative. It is notable that requests to see a solicitor declined as the age of detainees increased. For example, 56 per cent of under 16s asked for one (or might have been guided towards having one by an appropriate adult), while 38 per cent of those over 50 requested one. A significant minority, 10 per cent, neither requested nor declined a solicitor and this was usually occasioned by their being incapacitated in some way (most frequently by alcohol).

Appropriate adults

As we explore more fully in Chapter 6, appropriate adults have an important part to play in the care of detainees. Appropriate adults may be a parent or guardian, if they were not involved in the alleged offence for which the detainee was arrested, or an independent adult summoned by the police to assist the detainee. There are significant groups of detainees who need extra care and protection while in a police station: juveniles; the mentally disordered; and those with special needs. Just over 15 per cent of all detainees qualified for the assistance of an appropriate adult and, of those who did, the largest proportion – 62 per cent – were juveniles. Some of the juveniles also had multiple needs and so required a great deal of attention, which their immediate families were not always prepared or able to give. Those with special needs and/ or mental health problems comprised the remainder in roughly equal proportions.

Not all of the detainees assessed as requiring an appropriate adult actually saw one and the reasons for this were not always recorded. It was clear from the records that some were dealt with very quickly, with an appropriate adult responding by telephone rather than in person; some refused to attend at all; and some detainees themselves refused to have them. However, in almost a tenth of cases it was unclear why detainees that were eligible to see an appropriate adult did not do so.

PACE makes it absolutely clear that no action may be taken with a detainee requiring an appropriate adult, except in clearly defined circumstances, before an appropriate adult has arrived at the station. Bearing in mind the sometimes fragile physical and emotional state of some detainees, it is crucially important that they should not be detained longer than necessary.

Data were collected on cases in which it had taken more than four hours, from the time of having been summoned, for an appropriate adult to arrive at the station (presented in Table 3.6). This is quite a considerable period of time for a vulnerable detainee to wait for the detention procedures formally to begin. (Although any wait can be unacceptable, depending upon the age of the juvenile, we decided that four hours allowed for notification of an adult and travel to the station. Some adults have to arrange childcare or time off work before coming to the station.) At least a sixth of detainees (17 per cent) requiring an appropriate adult – and who actually saw one – had to wait more than four hours for one to arrive at the station. Juveniles comprised almost two-thirds of this group.

Table 3.6 Time taken for appropriate adult to arrive

Time taken	Number of detainees	Percentage
4–7 hours	106	56
8–11 hours	56	30
12–15 hours	18	10
16 hours or more	8	4
Total	188	100

Juveniles

PACE carefully delineates what may or may not be done with juveniles, and their care presents the police with particular responsibilities and concerns. Juveniles make up almost 10 per cent of all detainees.

Table 3.7 Comparison of ethnic origins of juvenile and adult detainees (%)

Ethnic origin	Juveniles	Adults
White European	29	34
Irish	4	12
Afro-Caribbean	57	40
Asian	5	7
Mediterranean	3	5
Oriental	1	*
Arabic	1	2

* Less than 1%

Table 3.7 shows that the ethnic origin of the juvenile 'population' in the custody suite during the period of the research differed somewhat from its adult equivalent. Thus, a significantly higher proportion of juveniles are Afro-Caribbean and a commensurately smaller proportion are White. Those identified by the police as being non-white (i.e. Afro-Caribbean, Asian, Mediterranean, Oriental or Arabic) comprise 67 per cent of the juvenile detainees, compared with a figure of 55 per cent police-identified non-white detainees overall and a demographic base of 54 per cent non-whites living in the local community.

We know from the data that some juveniles can wait a considerable time for an appropriate adult to arrive at the station. What is also clear is that some juveniles spend very long periods in detention, irrespective of when an appropriate adult arrives to see them at the station. The majority (65 per cent) were detained for no more than six hours, with a further 22 per cent being held for up to twelve hours. But 13 per cent were held for more than eighteen hours and just under 1 per cent were still in their detention room over 36 hours after first arriving at the station. Although we did not attempt to quantify this, it was clear from comparing the records of some of juveniles' co-accused that the juvenile was likely to be detained longer in the station for the same offence – and that this was attributable to the wait for an appropriate adult. The great majority of juveniles (92 per cent) were released back into the community, while 7 per cent were taken to court.

Predictably, there were some differences in reasons for arrest between adult and juvenile detainees (Table 3.8). Juveniles were more likely to be arrested for theft and handling offences and for criminal damage and burglary. They were much less likely to have been arrested for public order offences (often connected with drinking).

Table 3.8 Reasons for arrest (all detainees and juveniles) (%)

Major reasons for arrest	All detainees	Juveniles
Public order	22	8
Theft/handling	16	25
Criminal damage	6	10
Drugs	12	10
Violence	12	8
Motoring	9	1
Burglary*	4	9
Robbery*	5	20

Notes: totals do not add up to 100%

* categories additional to ones cited in Table 3.3

Strip searches

Having collected data from police records for the eight months prior to the installation of CCTV cameras and the nine months post-installation, we were able to check whether there had been any major change in the nature of the 'custodial population'. With one exception, which we come to below, any measurable differences were very minor and not of significance. Thus, for example, there was a slightly smaller proportion of Afro-Caribbeans brought to the cells in the post-installation period. However, this is much more likely to be a result of some of the changes taking place in relation to stop and search than anything happening in the police station. There was also a slight drop in drugs arrests. The major change pre- and post-installation, however, concerned the use of strip searches.

So far we have considered the make-up of the detained population passing through the police station. Within this overall group we have drawn attention to the very sizeable minority ethnic representation. In addition, we have looked at juveniles and others that might be considered to be particularly vulnerable, and examined basic features of their experience, such as how long they have to wait for an appropriate adult and how long they spend in custody. In considering the experience of prisoners in a police station there is one further very important element that is little talked about in the literature and yet, one may safely assume, is very significant to a minority of those kept in police custody. That is, strip searching.

At Kilburn in the seventeen months covered by the police records we examined we found that a total of 888 prisoners were strip-searched – representing 12 per cent of all detainees. There was a degree of gender difference, with 12 per cent of males and 7 per cent of females being strip-searched. However, the most significant difference concerns differences in the likelihood of being strip-searched according to ethnic origin (see Table 3.9).

Table 3.9 Proportion by ethnicity of detainees strip-searched (%)

Ethnicity	White European	Irish	Afro-Caribbean	Asian	Mediterranean	All
Proportion strip-searched	8	6	17	8	9	12

How might the significantly greater likelihood of Afro-Caribbeans being strip-searched be explained? One possible explanation might lie in the concentration of Afro-Caribbean prisoners charged with offences most likely to lead to a strip search being deemed necessary. Drugs offences were most likely to lead to a strip search – 46 per cent of such cases involving a strip search. In addition, one-fifth of suspects charged with robbery or with firearms offences were strip-searched and one-eighth of suspects charged with theft and handling offences (see Table 3.10).

Table 3.10 Proportion by charge of detainees strip-searched (%)

Offence	Proportion
Drugs	46
Firearms	21
Robbery	20
Theft/handling	12
Burglary	12

Indeed, Afro-Caribbean suspects were proportionately more likely to be charged with drugs offences than suspects of any other ethnic origin. However, this over-representation does not help account for the greater likelihood that Afro-Caribbean suspects will be strip-searched. Table 3.11 compares the likelihood of White European and Afro-Caribbean suspects being strip-searched according to the offence with which they were charged.

Table 3.11 Proportions by charge and ethnic origin of detainees strip-searched

Offence	Proportion		
	White European	Afro- Caribbean	All
Drugs	41	52	46
Robbery	11	22	20
Theft/handling	10	15	11
Burglary	7	18	12
Other	3	7	5

Note: total does not add up to 100%

Whichever way we consider it, therefore, Afro-Caribbean suspects are more likely to be strip-searched in police custody than suspects of other ethnic origins. The nature of their alleged offending cannot (fully) explain this disparity. This is clearly an area in which further investigation is required. However, it must be noted that the differential treatment suggested by the data is in line with allegations of discrimination brought to our attention by local community members during the course of the study.

Interestingly, it appears that the installation of CCTV had a measurable impact on the overall use of strip searches. In the period prior to the cameras being put in the cells 13 per cent of all prisoners were subject to a strip search. In the equivalent period after cameras had been installed the proportion dropped to 9 per cent. This is a reduction of over 30 per cent in the use of strip searches. This reduction appears not to affect particular ethnic groups disproportionately. Thus, although the proportion of Afro-Caribbean prisoners strip-searched fell from 20 per cent to 15 per cent after the cameras were installed, the equivalent figures for White prisoners for the same period were 10 per cent and 6 per cent. This was an unanticipated impact or consequence of the introduction of CCTV but, potentially, a very significant one.

Looking ahead to the Kilburn experiment

We have devoted a considerable part of this chapter to building up a picture of the detainees and understanding what happens to them at the station. We have looked at their reasons for arrest, ages, gender, ethnicity and the offences for which they were charged. Analysing the findings was complicated by the fact that so many records were incomplete, though not to the extent of significantly affecting the findings.

The data presented here provide the context in which to make sense of the use of CCTV cameras within the custody suite. We now have a clearer picture of what happens within a custody suite. We know more about who is arrested and brought to the station, and how long they are likely to remain. We now need to ask in what way the introduction of CCTV into the custody suite might affect detainees and those charged with their care.

It is clear that there are enormously diverse groups of detainees passing through any custody suite. Gender, age, ethnic origin and physical and mental health will all have an impact on the experience and understanding of detention. What does the addition of CCTV to a custody suite mean for the care of detainees? Inevitably, it means surveillance, but to what purpose? Through consideration of the groups passing through the custody suite, there is one immediate use for the cameras: as providers of a record.

- CCTV in the booking area of a custody suite can offer a record of the detainees' physical state as soon as they are within range of the cameras and, assuming detainees notice the cameras, this could be a reassurance for them.

- We have established that cell checks are not always consistent. The cameras would provide corroborative evidence of why checks might have been delayed – or whether they had taken place at all.

- The cameras in the corridors provide further corroborative evidence of who has been taken to a cell, or visited a cell, at a given time.

Once detainees have been charged and placed in the cells, the cameras can then assume another role; they become an additional means of monitoring detainees.

- The cameras can watch those at risk of self-harm, those with physical and/or mental health problems; the incapacitated (through drink or drugs); and the very young.

But this is to assume that the main purpose of the CCTV system is a benign one; providing the possibility of extra protection for detainees and, by extension, those responsible for them. It is possible that some of the groups we have examined – and many within all the groups – might not see the cameras in that light. Those subjected to a strip search in full view of the lens, for example, might have grave reservations. Those with mental health problems might see the cameras as a malign means of observation. Those obliged to spend disproportionate amounts of time in a cell might consider the surveillance overly intrusive. Having offered an overview of the client groups within a police custody suite, we now move beyond the quasi-anonymity of written records to the people themselves; the officers, the detainees and those charged with the care of detainees.

Notes

1 The cell cameras were first used on 21 January, 2000 and, where we refer to post-installation data, it relates to anything from this date.
2 We originally decided to identify all Irish detainees as a group distinct from other White Europeans because of their large local representation. Analysis of the data indicated that Irish prisoners were proportionately more likely to have been arrested for certain offences, such as public order, than were other White Europeans, but the overall differences were not significant.

Chapter 4

Watching and being watched

Our focus in this chapter is on the views and the experiences of the police officers working in the custody suite where this experiment took place. What did they think of the cameras? How did they think they affected detainees? How did cameras affect their own jobs? As we described in the first chapter, the role of the custody officer is one introduced by PACE. It is in some senses an unusual job in the police service for it involves being, in principle, an independent arbiter between suspects held in custody and officer colleagues who may wish to interview them. The extent to which custody officers are, in practice, actually able to divorce themselves from the broader values and priorities of police culture has been the subject of considerable debate (McConville *et al.* 1991; though see Dixon 1992). It is enough to note here that custody officers are subject to considerable pressure in their role (as we saw in Chapter 3), and that some of this stems from the position they occupy 'between' the suspect and the police service.

The custody officer has responsibility for the prisoners in their charge. They are assisted in these duties by 'gaolers', usually constables, who may undertake various duties in the custody suite up to and including the completion of the custody record (Bottomley *et al.* 1989). Central to the role of the custody sergeant is ensuring that suspects are aware of their rights in the police station. PACE requires that suspects be informed of their rights both verbally and in writing – in particular to have someone be informed of their arrest, to consult a solicitor and to see PACE *Codes of Practice*. The bulk of research suggests that custody officers largely comply with these requirements – though the delivery of spoken information has been found to affect the take-up of rights (Brown 1997).

The sample and the interviews

As we have already outlined, the interviews in this study were conducted in two stages. We did not select our sample by any predetermined rationale; any officer willing and free to be interviewed was interviewed. The first stage occurred prior to the installation of the cameras in the cells, but at a time when audio-linked cameras were already operating in the booking areas and cell corridors. A second and more extensive round of interviews was conducted after the cameras had been installed in the cells. A core of common questions was asked in both sets of interviews. They covered general experiences of working in the custody suite, impressions and experiences of the cameras operating in the booking area and cell corridors, and views about the anticipated and actual introduction of two systems of in-cell CCTV: a 'closed system' that could only be watched retrospectively, and an 'open system' that would be viewed in real time. The second set of interviews also focused on respondents' views and perceptions of the operation of the full-scale experiment; how the system was working in practice, and how it was experienced by those responsible for monitoring it, and for managing the custody suite.

During the pre-installation stage fourteen officers were interviewed, of whom nine were custody officers and five were gaolers. All were self-defined as White British and all but four were men. They had spent their entire service with the Metropolitan Police, with half having been officers for four to ten years and half for ten years and more. Twelve custody sergeants and three gaolers were interviewed after the cell cameras were installed. Three of those were women, and all but one were white, with that officer describing himself as African Caribbean. Their ages ranged from 27 to 42, with most being in their late 30s. The majority had served at least ten years in the police and, with one exception, had spent their entire careers in the Metropolitan Police, serving in various divisions. Overall, therefore, the sample consisted of 29 officers, seven of whom were women, and all but one of whom were white. For ease of description we will generally refer to both custody officers and gaolers simply as officers.

This chapter is based on data drawn from both sets of interviews. The views expressed by officers prior to the installation of cameras in the cells proved in practice to be little different from the views of other officers post-installation. As a consequence there is little to be gained by separating them and, for the most part, the interviews are treated as a single set[1].

The interviews were often conducted under difficult circumstances.

As with all the interviews in the study, respondents were assured of confidentiality. Somewhat ironically in the case of the officers, many of their interviews took place under the eye of the audio-linked CCTV cameras in the custody suite itself. The police station is very short of space and it was difficult to find an area that permitted a completely private interview. The officers' workload meant that they could not easily find the time to speak to the researcher and, understandably, most were reluctant to find time after their shifts had concluded. Interviews were sometimes curtailed and completed at a later date because staff were required back at the booking desk. Colleagues usually knew who was being interviewed and, at times, it must have been difficult for officers to speak as frankly as they might have wished. They had been encouraged to participate in the research, but had not been told explicitly that it was acceptable for them to take time off during shifts and the realities of the custody suite meant that doing so would not always have been easy. Colleagues frequently walked past the interview desk and there was always the knowledge that CCTV tapes might be viewed if there had been an incident in the custody suite that needed further explanation.

A few officers were very wary of committing themselves to a formal interview – and were also unhappy about releasing colleagues from their duties so that they could be interviewed. As officers grew accustomed to seeing the researcher in the suite most became more forthcoming. There is a disparity, however, between the number of gaolers and sergeants who were interviewed. Gaolers are not a mandatory addition to the custody team and, when they are included in the shift, their services are much in demand. This is reflected in the few who were available for interview. Gaolers are also under pressure because some are relatively new to the job and often need extra supervision from the sergeants. Their relative inexperience may have meant that some lacked the confidence to push to be allowed to be interviewed.

Working in a stressful environment

In the light of the interview difficulties they faced, officers spoke remarkably frankly. Often, it was with a degree of rancour about their working environment. The custody suite was rebuilt in 1991 and, until the end of 1999, had no external ventilation. Extremes of temperature were common, both within the cells and the custody area. The suite was cramped and there was often a queue of people, waiting to be attended to, milling around the booking desk. Both the custody and the bailed-to-return desks provided insufficient space. The bailed-to-return desk, in particular, offered no protection to staff.

The Health and Safety aspects aren't looked at. The first two months I worked here I got lots of colds and stomach complaints because of the people we come into contact with. TB is a big concern. This winter everyone got the flu – we don't get jabs.

(CO 3)

Most frequently they spoke about the pressures of their work and being undervalued. As has earlier been outlined in some detail, the role of the custody officer is multi-faceted. The procedural structures of their work are defined by PACE, yet officers are required to exercise their authority and discretion within a highly stressful environment.

[Management] are very lax on a number of areas – which is put down to the fact that Kilburn is busier than others. This is no excuse ... I always have to search for things which should be readily accessible. In a very busy suite there should be better management. I am forced to breach *Codes* [PACE *Codes of Practice*] continually to allow the job to work.

(pre CO 1)

Management is not aware of the pressures, hence the terrible conditions in which we work.

(pre CO 4)

Officers are expected to adhere to high standards of professionalism, while coping with staff shortages, working in an ill-designed custody suite, facing distressed and sometimes abusive detainees, as well as coping with the professional demands of others such as solicitors and doctors. Officers may be required to mop down a floor because a detainee has vomited, urinated or defecated in the public parts of the custody area. They might need to deal with a severely claustrophobic detainee or find the time to talk to a frightened – and aggressive – child whose parents have refused to come to the station. Cell checks must be made hourly and some may be half- or quarter-hourly, because a detainee is thought to be 'at risk'. The cell buzzers might be ringing, with detainees wanting water, toilet paper, food, information about the whereabouts of their solicitor or interpreter – or just some human contact, because they are afraid. The cells may be full – and there are seventeen at Kilburn – yet staff also have to ensure that the written records are accurate and up to date. Most officers thought (probably quite correctly) that the public at large had no conception of the types of situations they were obliged to deal with.

It is a most stressful position, dealing with prisoners, solicitors, immigration, drug referrals. There is no scope for error. They are intent on making you do more and that is a big responsibility. If I authorised a search of a juvenile, without realising he was a juvenile, I would not necessarily get support.

(pre CO 9)

Officers distinguished between the levels of support they felt they received from different colleagues. In particular, those who had experienced the role themselves were understandably empathetic, even while preoccupied with their own work.

I have good support from custody officers and also from arresting officers. It can get very busy and if they're juggling many things, then a lot falls to the gaoler. Also, the area can get very warm and stuffy because there is no ventilation. When it's busy there is less support for the gaoler.

(pre G 2)

The sergeants are all supportive. Those who have done it are in general supportive, but if they're in a rush people tend to prioritise their own interests.

(pre CO 2)

Despite some occasional difficulties, however, the officers interviewed did not feel that pressure from immediate colleagues led to any serious problems in complying with PACE. Indeed, they appeared proud of, and were explicit in descriptions of their common professionalism in this regard.

The environment here is that you need everybody to help out. There are complex areas of PACE to deal with and you need their co-operation. Practically, it's impossible to oversee everything, so you need to be able to rely on other officers.

(CO 12)

You are constantly having to be impartial. You must deal with the person by the book. It is difficult if a colleague has been assaulted and you do not appear to be supporting them. It is imperative that the custody sergeant should be seen to be impartial. When you discuss it later, colleagues understand.

(pre CO 9)

Officers were less certain that other colleagues understood their prime responsibility to abide by PACE and drew a distinction between those in uniform (and, by implication, at the 'coal face' of policing) and those not.

> There is conflict with the CID regarding PACE regulations. They are so preoccupied with their investigations and it's unclear whose responsibility it is to investigate prisoners. The uniformed officers are very supportive.
>
> (pre CO 7)

In addition to all these responsibilities, under PACE *Codes of Practice*, officers are required to call the police surgeon immediately if a detainee appears to be physically or mentally ill, injured, unconscious or semi-conscious, behaving abnormally or otherwise in need of medical attention. This provision has had the effect of increasing substantially the proportion of cases in which police surgeons are called, though there remains considerable variation between stations (Brown 1989; Robertson 1992). The highest rates are found in the Metropolitan Police, and as we saw in Chapter 3, there were very high rates at Kilburn at the time of the research. We explored with officers their practices in this regard. The consensus among officers was that there existed a presumption in favour of calling the FME, rather than 'having to justify a refusal to call' (pre CO 7). In essence, they sometimes felt that they could not risk failing to call them.

> If I'm in doubt I call them out. I won't be criticised for calling a doctor but might be for not calling them. No it's not difficult. It can be time-consuming for a gaoler.
>
> (pre CO 2)

> Not personally. If I feel the FME is required I will call them. I can speak to them on the phone first and get advice. With asthmatics that is possible. If it was a juvenile I would always call the FME. Checking is sometimes difficult, when you are very busy. Provided you have a system running it can be done.
>
> (CO 7)

> Discretion has been removed entirely from [custody] officers, which is a dreadful situation. Financially it is ludicrous. FMEs are called easily just to protect yourself. We are responsible people who should be able to take responsibility. Huge money is spent on FMEs. I call him far too frequently, just to cover ourselves in terms of criticism.
>
> (pre CO 1)

Officers also suggested that some of this apparent overuse of FMEs was prompted by detainees who were likely to want to see 'the doctor at the drop of a hat given the opportunity – nine out of ten times they wouldn't go to a doctor if they weren't in custody' (pre CO 3) – and that some were in 'fear of cold turkey in the cell, so they request[ed] a doctor every ten minutes' (pre CO 5).

Getting the work done

Officers will never know precisely what they may be called on to deal with during each shift, but one task remains fixed, and that is the checking of cells. The PACE *Codes of Practice* stipulate that detainees must be visited every hour and, should the detainee be drunk, every half-hour, when they must be roused and spoken to (C8.10). As section C8A clarifies, 'juveniles and other people at risk should be visited more frequently' and, for these detainees, police practice is normally to make quarter-hourly checks. Should a gaoler be part of the shift team, this will be their responsibility.

> If we are very busy or dealing with violent offenders, when you need your accompanying officer to carry out a check. If you have to do frequent checks – such as for drunks – it can be very difficult to carry them out as properly as it should be. The checks are very important.
>
> (pre G 2)

> When the board is full it's a nightmare to keep up to date with the checks. I would rely on the gaolers to keep up to speed.
>
> (CO 2)

> It depends on the number of prisoners, especially if quarter-hour checks are required on a number. You have the needs of individual prisoners, their meals...I am responsible for property – it takes a good half-hour to check through the bag on the changeover.
>
> (pre G 5)

As this last quote illustrates, officers are often faced with negotiating a complex set of demands, requests, needs and rights. Officers have to do this in an environment which is often hectic and generally unpredictable.

> Sometimes there are only two of you, but lots of prisoners. Yesterday there were six to seven juveniles, so there was a need for an appropriate adult [in each case]. One kicks the door – others

Plate 1 A cell corridor, with two cameras visible on the ceiling (photo courtesy of *Héloïse Hayman*)

kick the door. Prisoners will feign sickness. They will block toilets and flood cells. Sometimes they are too violent and charges have to be read through the wicket [a trapdoor in the cell door]. The bell is sometimes disengaged if it all gets too hectic and someone is repeatedly seeking attention.

(pre CO)

Here, the officer reveals that one way of coping with demanding detainees is to 'isolate' the buzzer that enables them to request attention from within in the cell. Though this did not appear to occur as a matter of routine, during the course of our research it was a tactic resorted to by several officers.

You get the buzzers going, generally from those in longer – purely just to speak to someone.

(CO 2)

[They want] telephone calls, visits by relatives, cigarettes. It depends how busy we are. If we are *very* busy we will sometimes isolate the buzzer, but we will continue to monitor them.

(CO 5)

Detainees may make many different requests, often simply to be allowed to smoke or just to be out of the cells for a while. However, the opportunities to allow such requests are strictly limited.

Some suffer from claustrophobia. I do not have the resources to allow them to sit out of the cell. The constant asking for cigarettes is very annoying. There are no facilities for allowing smoking. All the police areas are non-smoking. There can be a fire risk in the cells.

(pre CO 9)

Nevertheless, opportunities are found to allow detainees to smoke, and making allowances in this regard can be one way in which order is negotiated within the custody suite.

Invariably calls are just for a smoke and that depends on the officer. I don't mind letting them smoke as that keeps them more contented. I'd let them smoke if I had CCTV, as then I could see that they have not set things alight.

(pre CO 7)

Keeping watch

When officers were asked how aware they were of the cameras in the booking area during the course of their work, only four said that they were completely unaware of them. The fact that the majority were keenly aware of the cameras' presence does not imply, however, that they were overly concerned by them. By the time of these interviews (conducted once the cameras had been in the booking area for several months), most had become accustomed to a high level of surveillance in the booking area and adapted their working habits to accommodate it. The cameras had become part of their everyday life and were registered almost subconsciously. In the following quotes the officers describe the perceived impact of the cameras on both their own and detainees' behaviour.

When I first came here I was very aware – it's like someone in a glass window standing above you. Like a rat in a trap. It now doesn't bother me. When I first came in I watched everything I said – now I don't.

(G 3)

My level of awareness goes up and down, depending upon the circumstances. I am always very aware when a difficult prisoner is brought in, partly because I always tell them they are being recorded. Sometimes it modifies their behaviour, sometimes it reassures them.

(CO 12)

To begin with, very aware, but now 'aware'. If you are having conversations and are rude about other officers you say 'sorry mate, didn't mean that', to the cameras. It has inhibited certain things – there's not as much swearing. Officers in this enlightened day and age are scared to say the wrong thing, without meaning to. It's maybe not such a bad thing, as it makes them aware.

(CO 9)

In the main, by contrast, when asked how they thought detainees responded to the booking area cameras, officers were largely sceptical of any modification of behaviour.

The majority don't care. Some are aware – even though you tell them, they don't care. If they want to be abusive they will be.

(CO 11)

Often they are not aware of it. I draw it to their attention if they are behaving badly and sometimes it will calm some people down, but if they are drunk or on drugs it may make no difference.

(pre CO 5)

The low-key attitude towards cameras in the booking area and the cell corridors was reinforced in custody officers' and gaolers' accounts of how they 'monitored' the screens. The expectation at this stage was not that the screen would be continuously monitored; rather, that it would be used when the custody officer deemed it necessary to do so. Indeed, the view from the gaolers was that the custody officers did not spend much time at all watching the screen. In part this was because it was positioned in such a way as to make it easier for the gaolers to watch it 'automatically', and in part they were either too busy or did not consider it important. (Following the introduction of the cell cameras the monitor was repositioned, behind the backs of the sergeants, making it even more unlikely that it would be observed consistently.) To a degree this was reflected in custody sergeants' own accounts which were dominated by a notion of watching 'only when it's necessary'.

> There is not that much information on it. If there is a noise from up one corridor you may use it to see what is happening up there. I only use it for specific reasons, for deliberate usage, not just in passing.
>
> (pre G 3)

Indeed, at this stage there was relatively little sense that the purpose of cameras in the custody suite was expected to be monitory. Despite officers mentioning that they looked at the cameras to check that colleagues were not in difficulty, no officers said that they felt that their colleagues were watching and protecting them during the course of their duties.

> I tend to forget about them. There never seems to be a reason to look at it. Occasionally, if there is a gaoler in the cell passage and I think there may be trouble, I look at it.
>
> (pre CO 5)

> It's not very interesting! You might want to look if someone has gone down the cell passageway.
>
> (CO 6)

> I am usually too busy doing everything else. We are not expected to sit and monitor that screen. That would be a full-time job.
>
> (pre CO 3)

Ensuring professionalism

When discussing the booking area surveillance several officers mentioned the cameras' potential benefits to detainees, but explaining this potential was not always straightforward. The impact of the cameras, like the impact of other 'crime prevention' measures, often concerned the *absence*, rather than the presence, of something. To the extent that something discernible had happened as a result of the introduction of cameras, according to officers it concerned the 'professionalism' of their colleagues in the custody suite.

[Police officers] have to act in as close accordance with the *Codes* as possible. I would not be so concerned with the immediacy of checks etc. They ensure things are done in time, as opposed to just when we have the time. They assist with the integrity of property, possibly. I have never heard of this happening in any case, but CCTV should reduce this more.

(pre CO 1)

It makes arresting officers and others behave in a much more professional manner, that they stick to the book. When under pressure from violent prisoners it is a help.

(pre CO 5)

We are professional people and take pride in our professional [behaviour]. Force sometimes has to be used with violent prisoners but CCTV doesn't really affect this except as a source of evidence afterwards to show how it started.

(pre G 3)

Officers believed that the cameras both altered and inhibited their conversations with detainees and each other and, as one put it, there was 'less pushing the margins' as a consequence.

It makes them a bit more careful about what they say. Once, if someone had come in screaming and shouting, they might have been pushed into a chair and told to keep quiet. Now it doesn't happen. I think it's a good thing.

(G 3)

Other officers were more sceptical about whether the cameras had had this impact. All were convinced that there was a greater degree of 'professionalism' visible in the work conducted in the custody suite than there had been in previous times. However, some argued that this had been brought about by other means, and had certainly occurred before the cameras were introduced.

While it could arguably be said that enhancing professional standards is probably the most visible of the benefits conferred by the cameras (according to officers' own accounts), perhaps the most keenly felt change was the impact of the cameras on the 'privacy' of officers. Whilst regretting the loss of privacy, officers also acknowledged that the cameras forced them to confront their own standards of behaviour when at work. Their concerns were not related to the visual monitoring of the suite itself, but the fact that their 'private' conversations were recorded. Put bluntly, they felt that they could not say the sorts of things in the custody suite that they might say in the pub (and by implication had once said in the custody suite) and a few were aggrieved by the loss of what they had previously thought of as little more than idle banter.

> ...my right to a private conversation with my colleagues has gone and that is an invasion of my privacy. I still monitor my behaviour as a police officer but cameras do invade my privacy.
>
> (CO 4)

> When I'm alone, I'm not alone. If I'm picking my nose I'm conscious of how far up I stick my finger. If I want to be flippant to a prisoner I'm conscious it may be construed as more than just a flippant remark.
>
> (pre G 4)

Here, custody officers and gaolers are giving expression to the feeling that their purely 'private' conversations could be listened to by other (senior) officers. This they resent and feel to be intrusive. As a direct consequence, officers will now sometimes conduct conversations about detainees in one of the rooms not covered by cameras, because they do not wish to be overheard. Indeed, it is worth reinforcing the point that it is the recording of sound that primarily concerns officers. Little concern was expressed about the recording of visual images. Rather, the reverse. Officers found the existence of a visual record generally reassuring.

Cameras as guarantors of safety

While officers had regrets for the loss of a more relaxed working environment, they welcomed the evidential and retrospective capabilities of the cameras. They saw them as a protection for themselves, but were quick to make clear that they were not referring to their physical safety.

> Safety regarding 'having a go' doesn't worry me. As far as allegations are concerned, yes. I was dealing with someone with learning difficulties and he said he was forced to sign, but the CCTV showed differently.
>
> (CO 4)

> It makes me feel more secure because of the occasional malicious allegation. It doesn't make me feel more physically secure.
>
> (CO 5)

67

The system is more for recording what is happening rather than for me to look at. I know what is going on anyway. It's there to safeguard you from any allegation, but it has no role in the day-to-day running of the station.

(pre CO 6)

This sense of the cameras' evidential worth was reinforced by officers' experience of the impact of cameras in the booking area and cell corridors on the behaviour of detainees. The majority of officers felt that there was minimal impact, apart from the occasional realisation that the tape might hold incriminating evidence.

They calm down. If they fail to calm down immediately, after time in the cells they come out and apologise because they are concerned you might show someone the tape.

(CO 3)

The majority don't care. Some are aware – even though you tell them, they don't care. If they want to be abusive they will be.

(CO 11)

That said, some officers did suggest that even though most detainees' behaviour might not be affected by the CCTV, on occasion the existence of the cameras did prevent allegations of police misconduct being made, further contributing to the protection of the officers.

They have withdrawn accusations after being told about the cameras. For example, smashing their watch then alleging that the police did it.

(pre CO 8)

Indeed, officers also suggested that where allegations had not been withdrawn, evidence from the 'cameras ha[d] been used in prosecutions to refute allegations' (CO 9).

Consensus on the booking area cameras?

Overall, officers were very positive about the use of CCTV in the booking areas and cell corridors in the custody suite. As we have outlined, there were initial fears about the presence of the cameras that were largely dispelled as officers became accustomed to the new technology. Their somewhat muted reservations about loss of personal privacy remained, but these were outweighed by the considerable benefits of protection –

not necessarily from assault, but more specifically against unfounded or malicious complaints. Officers generally regarded the system as an important safeguard, both for themselves and the detainees for whom they were responsible.

> It's excellent. More places should have it. I'd even go so far as to say they should be in cars and vans. The behaviour of the police is generally so much better, they are observed by the public. The cameras would prevent allegations.
>
> (pre CO 9)

> They're a very good idea in that they protect all parties – police, prisoners and anyone else who works there – from false allegations and improper behaviour.
>
> (CO 10)

> I'm no less likely to be attacked by suspects – most are 'high' or unaware. But I'm much safer in terms of factual representation of events and therefore protected from false allegation.
>
> (pre CO 7)

The only respondent to mention any other form of impact was a gaoler who suggested that there might be wider public benefits. CCTV cameras, he suggested, were 'good for the reassurance of the public because it tells them exactly what is happening in a realistic way' (pre G 1). As we outlined earlier, such public reassurance was one of the central motives for the later introduction of the full-scale CCTV experiment in Kilburn. Given that, it is revealing that only one officer mentioned it.

Anticipating in-cell cameras

When asked to think ahead and anticipate what the introduction of in-cell cameras might mean, officers were concerned that they would only serve to increase the number of tasks they were expected to undertake and, consequently, would increase the pressure they were under. The first point that most officers made was that, although they would be able to look at a monitor from time to time, the nature of their job would preclude continuous monitoring of the screen. Nonetheless, they believed that they would be the ones expected to monitor the images relayed from the cells (especially in view of the sensitivity of the information and the issue of privacy) should the cameras be introduced.

On the assumption that they could not be expected to do this work – and they believed there was little point in having the cameras in the cells unless they were continuously monitored – a question arose as to how it should be covered. The only answer they could arrive at was that such an experiment, if it were to work, would require the addition of new dedicated staff who would be able to watch the screens continuously.

> There's no time for the custody officer to monitor [the screens]. It would need another officer just to look at the monitor.
>
> (pre CO 4)

> If someone could monitor it permanently, other than the custody sergeant, then I'd be very much in favour of it.
>
> (pre CO 5)

However, whilst in principle this appeared to them to be the solution to the problem, none thought that such staff would be available in practice.

> I don't see how it would work without a dedicated officer. When we're busy it would be impossible to watch it as often necessary to make it work. [However] I don't see 'the job' [the force] providing a dedicated officer.
>
> (pre CO 1)

As a consequence, custody officers were particularly concerned about what they assumed would be not only an increase in their workload, but also an extension of their responsibilities and, therefore, liabilities.

> I cannot monitor a screen continuously, so it would just be something else I would not be able to do properly and would get into trouble for.
>
> (pre CO 5)

Officers were shortly to discover the accuracy of their predictions. A considerable amount of money was spent installing the cameras, but no extra resources were made available for extra staff to monitor the screens. In the event, the existing custody staff were expected to keep an eye on the monitor while carrying out all their other duties.

The Protocols

As we have already seen, officers had anticipated both that the cameras would increase their responsibilities and that no extra staff would be forthcoming to help them cope. Worries about their new role led staff to request that their responsibilities should be specified and, after consultation with the Police Federation, a series of Protocols were provided (reproduced in the Appendix), all 'supporting the recommendations of the Police Complaints Authority' (PCA 1999).[2]

These emphasised that the cameras were not to replace the 'normal methods of prisoner care', including regular checks, and that the system should 'enhance the care already available'. Risk assessment forms were still to be completed and monitors could be viewed by 'FMEs and qualified psychiatric teams' if they assisted in the assessment of detainees' mental health. Lay visitors were specifically barred from viewing the monitors, but could have access to the tapes 'on the authority of the Operational Command Unit Commander in order to prevent serious public disorder'.[3] The Protocols also defined who had responsibility for the tapes and how these should be changed and sealed following use. The avoidance of any voyeurism, occasioned by the cameras, was made the responsibility of the custody officers. There were no limitations imposed on cross-gender viewing of the monitors; male staff could observe female detainees and vice versa.

The specific concern about who should do the monitoring, and how often, was addressed by Protocol Three, which states: *There is no requirement for the custody staff to view the CCTV monitors on a constant basis.* Although pleased that their concerns had been heeded, the end result was viewed with some scepticism by officers.

> If something *did* happen though, you would be asked *why* you didn't see it – and you could be snowed under at the time. [This interviewee had not seen the Protocol almost two months after the cameras were first used.]
>
> (CO 2)

> Whatever the Protocol is, it will always come down to what is going on at the time.
>
> (CO 8)

From the outset then, although the cameras were present, they were not, at least so far as official station policy was concerned, a constant, monitoring and monitored presence. Resources had not been made available to ensure that the screens would be watched at all times. What was left unspecified, and clearly of concern to custody suite staff, was precisely what the expectation was. How frequently were the monitors to be watched? There was a sense of uneasy tension between the 'official' position encapsulated in the Protocol, that allowed for occasional monitoring of the cameras, and the broader sense that if something should go wrong – and officers had not been watching the screen – there would be relatively little sympathy for them if they said that at the time they were too busy.

Training

Some officers interviewed during the first round of interviews suggested that the new enterprise might well require extra training. As with the majority of their other comments about CCTV, this observation was made in support of the extension of the system, but also with an awareness of its implications.

> Systems are only as effective as the people who are monitoring them. [You need] training and good staff…Staff have to be much more trained and better and on the ball.
>
> (pre CO 1)

Although there had been some general discussion with the custody staff about the introduction of the cell cameras, little specific training was provided and officers often learned from each other how to operate the monitors. As has already been noted, at least one of the officers had not been shown the Protocols before starting to monitor the cameras.

> [I had] very little training, although it's a simple system. I am unsure about switching to the 'spot' camera [the camera used for surveillance of especially vulnerable prisoners]. It's a question of playing about with it, but formal instruction would have been handy – or a set of written instructions. You can turn the screens off.
>
> (CO 5)

> [I received] about four minutes from the custody officer I was taking over from.
>
> (CO 12)

> I would like some training so I can use it effectively and properly. I don't know *exactly* what I can do. I don't know what all the other buttons do.
>
> (CO 8)

While custody officers supported each other, they appeared distrustful of senior management, who were frequently criticised as being remote and

Plate 2 Custody desk, as seen by detainees. The cell monitors are in the middle, between the computers. The monitor for the rest of the custody suite is on the back wall, next to the window (photo courtesy of Héloïse Hayman)

out of touch – though the senior officer with primary responsibility for the custody suite at the time of the experiment was exempted from such criticism. It was felt that new procedures were introduced by senior staff, with little understanding being shown of how these might affect the custody officers' workload.

> We all suffer from lack of training, lack of supervision. There is nobody to turn to – everyone feels very isolated and it's dangerous.
>
> (CO 3)

> There's a whole tier of management I could walk past and not recognise. They don't come down here often enough. It's out of sight, out of mind.
>
> (CO 6)

With the number of 'teams' staffing the custody suite (each containing six sergeants and four gaolers), their varying shift patterns and changing personnel as new officers arrived at the station, information was not always relayed adequately and quickly enough. (A minor example of this lack of communication was the fact that a number of officers did not realise that a researcher would be in the custody suite during the course of this evaluation.) Having to contend with unfamiliar equipment, and make decisions as to its best use, complicated what was frequently a very full workload. When available, gaolers carried out cell checks and updated records, changed tapes, responded to cell buzzers, provided meals and checked in property. In their absence, custody sergeants were required to undertake those duties. Staff also had to arrange medical examinations; call for appropriate adults, social workers and interpreters; respond to solicitors' queries; answer the constant telephone calls, all while completing custody records and continually adding to them during the suspect's detention. Quite frequently the bailed-to-return desk was not staffed because of staff shortages, and all bailees were directed to the booking desk, further increasing the workload. Officers needed to know immediately the capabilities of their new CCTV monitors – and many did not.

Cameras in the cells

The cameras in the 'public areas' appeared to have become somewhat like part of the furniture. Officers were aware of their presence, felt that they had had an impact on the culture of the custody suite; and yet the cameras were not a preoccupation. By contrast, the cell cameras could not be so easily ignored, not least because they so visibly demanded the officers' attention, even if they had relatively little time to bestow it. Additionally, there was the matter of the camera positioned above the booking desk to ensure that voyeurism did not take place, which left the officers scrutinised as never before. Having managed to compartmentalise the old cameras as a necessary, if not always welcome, adjunct to their work, they were now faced with an unavoidable reminder of the presence of CCTV. This had an impact in two ways. Firstly, it raised general awareness and reminded officers that the CCTV needed to be monitored on a regular basis. Secondly, it provided a visible reminder that they themselves were being watched – indeed was unwelcome evidence that some senior officers felt they might not be trusted to behave in a professional manner at all times.

During the first interview stage officers suggested that they were already under huge pressure and that CCTV in the cells might help to relieve that (although, as we have shown, there was a concomitant view that it would increase the pressure). It was also felt that the cameras would corroborate the written record, by showing whether or not cells had been checked as indicated and just who had entered cells at various points. While most believed that the PACE requirements regarding the timing of actual cell visits should still be adhered to, there were some that wondered if the monitors might not suffice for some of the checks.

With continuous recording you have access. If someone kicks on the cell door then goes quiet, you can check nothing untoward is happening. It is not always practicable to visit immediately, so continuous recording is an extra safeguard.

(pre CO 9)

CCTV doesn't help with checks on drunks, but it does with those who are suicidal. I would question the need for quarter-hour checks now the cameras are in place. I could put an entry in the custody record – 'CCTV monitored'.

(G 1)

The additional cameras emphasised that the space which had previously appeared to be 'theirs', even while under video surveillance, was truly a public arena and that their every action and comment was potentially open to scrutiny. In much the same way that detainees would have to come to terms with the loss of what little privacy they had in the cells, officers had to adjust to this new reality; virtually nowhere in the custody suite could be their private domain. As we have noted, this had the effect of encouraging some to retire to the property room, which lacked a camera, where it was not uncommon for officers to gather to discuss things which they did not wish to have recorded. Even then, the cameras would record their entry into the room – and who accompanied them – and they knew they might be required to account for themselves if the need arose. On some occasions they adjourned to other parts of the station.

Officers are probably more careful about how they express themselves in the custody area. Generally, they wouldn't want to say anything that could provide ammunition in court. Feelings will be voiced elsewhere.

(CO 12)

You look at the notes and see things have been left out and you go to the little room and they'll explain why. They don't want to say something on camera.

(CO 11)

Above all, however, they seemed to have accepted that there was a rationale for the use of cameras in the custody suite, and most were ready for the next step.

This is a natural progression for us. We had gone halfway. Now we have gone the rest of the journey.

(CO 1)

Becoming accustomed

Officers gradually became more accustomed to the technical requirements of the booking desk monitors, although some found the multiple-image screen hard to follow and considered it unsatisfactory. A number began to articulate concerns about what they were required to view and some felt profoundly uncomfortable with their new role.

I was on night duty eight weeks ago and I didn't know how to change the 'spot' camera. I had not been trained. A guy was on the loo and I couldn't turn him off. I turned away because he took so long and I didn't want to watch. Recently someone was masturbating and I turned him off [i.e. turned off the 'spot' camera; the cameras cannot be turned off completely]. I rarely watch the screen.

(CO 4)

It seems intrusive, to be honest. I would rather not see them on the toilet. There is no dignity involved in a strip search. Last week I watched someone drink water out of the toilet.

(G 2)

Some talked explicitly about the likely impact on detainees.

There are issues of privacy – but they don't have it, really because we can open the door whenever we want. If drugs are concealed upon their person this will hopefully put a stop to that. Very few women are strip-searched.[4] I would hope that the police are professional enough not to watch. Having a room without a video is no answer if there is a false allegation – you take them to the one cell that doesn't have a camera and it doesn't look good.

(CO 1)

I'm surprised it wasn't made obvious to the prisoners that the cameras were there. It is not required that they be told, in the Protocol. The vast majority ignore it. Some don't – they chuck things, they shout. They think it's a way of keeping in touch with the COs. I know it's not linked to audio – others don't.

(CO 5)

As the detainees themselves were also to do, custody officers focused particularly on the fact that the toilet was not hidden from view. This, they felt, posed the greatest concern in relation to detainees' privacy. Indeed, one custody sergeant felt so strongly about this that he felt it completely undermined the legitimacy of in-cell CCTV.

> I think it is right and proper in the custody suite and all passages, though it deprives me of my privacy. But I am strongly opposed to its use in cells because it is an invasion of detainees' privacy. The only way to stop them injuring themselves is by total vigilance in searching or monitoring and in doctor's checks.
>
> (pre CO 4)

Officers questioned the extent of the camera's gaze and its necessity. Primarily, they were concerned about the toilet areas and the fact that they were in a position to view something intensely private. They wanted a means of switching the screen off, but also wanted recording to continue so that there would be an uninterrupted record of the suspect's detention. Most said that they would turn away if they became aware that the toilet was being used but, on the 'spot' screen especially, the image could be large and would catch them unawares if they had been dealing with other things.

> [I would like an] on/off switch so they don't think we're 'getting off' watching them being stripped or going to the toilet. If we have it for evidence you can't blank it out – so we'll get sued on a test case.
>
> (G 2)

> The cameras shouldn't cover the toilet areas. It's degrading – people are innocent until proven guilty. People should be searched properly and then there wouldn't be the worry about evidence being flushed away.
>
> (CO 11)

> There is an unavoidable problem around decency. I can't see any way around it. Most COs deal with it by not staring at the cameras when someone is on the toilet.
>
> (CO 12)

Strip searches

Cells are not used simply to detain prisoners. They are also used for strip searches and, as we discussed in Chapter 3, approximately 12 per cent of male detainees and 7 per cent of female detainees undergo them. Of these, approximately 10 per cent are juveniles. The cameras record the searches and they are seen on the monitor. Under PACE, there are strict regulations detailing who may be present during strip searches, depending upon the sex of the detainee.

The PACE *Codes of Practice* (Annexe A) stipulate that:

11(a) a police officer carrying out a strip search must be of the same sex as the person searched;

11(b) the search shall take place in an area where the person being searched cannot be seen by anyone who does not need to be present, nor by a member of the opposite sex (except an appropriate adult who has been specifically requested by the person being searched).

Further:

11(e) where necessary to assist the search, the person may be required ... to bend forward so that a visual examination may be made of the genital and anal areas provided that no physical contact is made with any body orifice.

Although viewing of the monitors is restricted to custody staff, there is no restriction upon cross-gender viewing, a matter of concern to staff.

A loss of dignity occurs when you put them in a cell in the first place and this would exacerbate that, particularly where someone of the opposite sex is being watched.

(pre G 3)

Consequently, male staff are in a position to view women being stripped as may female staff view men being stripped. The degree to which staff may view a detainee, especially when that person is required to bend forward in order to facilitate the search, raises various questions, not least regarding the reaction of those who are actually searched. Research on women in prison shows that they frequently find such searches traumatic, particularly 'given the histories of sexual abuse and assault that many ... bring with them' (Chesney-Lind 1997). At this stage in the life of the Kilburn experiment, and having sought legal opinion, the police were of the view that the fact that strip searches are seen at a remove absolves them of the PACE requirements.[5] Staff, nevertheless, were left feeling very discomforted.

The only concern I have is with female prisoners. The privacy side of things – females on the toilet and occasions when somebody is under treatment at a mental institution. But then it's the same for female officers with male detainees. For strip searches I would switch off the camera [meaning he would switch from multiple- to single-screen mode on the main monitor]. I wouldn't look at the cameras. I would like to be able to switch the camera off in those circumstances – but perhaps the FME's room can be used [as it does not contain a camera]

(CO 7)

There is also the question of the officers' interpretation of actions they see on the monitor. For example, a female suspect might be changing a tampon, but this could be assumed to be the secretion or removal of drugs and might conceivably lead to the unnecessary strip searching of the detainee.

It is important, as with so much of this experiment in surveillance, to note that issues of privacy cannot be understood in isolation from questions of protection. Thus, it might be argued that the cameras provide an extra degree of protection during strip searches as they provide a record of how the search was conducted. This record is of equal value to the detainees and the officers, showing if there has been an assault or inappropriate handling of the suspect or, indeed, potentially disproving allegations of such behaviour. Whether this intention would survive a legal challenge is, of course, yet to be discovered. In the United States it has already been put to the test within the context of imprisonment. Wall-mounted video monitors were installed in some New York state prisons in areas where strip searches were carried out, largely to counter complaints by males that they had been beaten during searches. When videoing of strip searches began at Albion Correctional Center, a women's prison, the fixed cameras were replaced by hand-held ones and a number of women filed complaints, which eventually led to the ending of routine videotaping of women prisoners being strip-searched. Moreover, it led to a change of policy in that a woman could only be taped if it was believed that she would resist a search (Chesney-Lind 1997).

Protection – for whom?

As can already be seen, privacy was one of the first casualties of the cameras. Perhaps an inevitable casualty when considered at this remove, but its loss had an impact on staff because they were subject to it almost as much as any of the detainees. They had been brought face to face with their own public role, having previously cherished what might have been the illusion that they were working within a partially private domain. Nothing that they undertook within the entire custody suite was beyond the gaze of the cameras. In a sense, they became partners of the detainees in the enterprise. Staff could not turn off the cameras focused on themselves; detainees, similarly, could not turn off the cameras, nor request that this be done on their behalf. Both groups were also partners in the other half of the enterprise, that of providing protection, even if one group continued to have authority over the other.

When the cell cameras were officially launched on 14 March 2000, the Borough Commander said that the 'CCTV scheme [would] allow for complete transparency of police treatment of prisoners, enhance prisoner care and improve community confidence in Brent Police' (*The Job*, 24 March 2000). While staff might have felt that they already protected detainees to the best of their ability, this was not always the public perception.

Transparency was clearly central, but the question of who needed protection from whom, insofar as staff were concerned, was not fully dealt with in the public debate. Publicly, the emphasis was on the protection of detainees: from assault; from self-harm, and from the consequences of medical emergencies. Within the station there was a much more explicit acceptance of the fact that the protection offered by the cameras could be extended to the police as well as to detainees. Reflecting on this, a senior member of management later commented, 'we also need to be able to afford protection to our officers, because the feeling of guilt when something does go wrong...must be tremendous. We need to protect the officers. We also want to be able to deliver the duty of care' (Interview, September 2000: 2). Officers were clearly concerned about the possibility of false allegations, wanted professional security, and believed that the cameras would help deliver this.

It doesn't make me feel safer from physical attack, but it does regarding allegations.

(CO 11)

[It makes me feel safer from] allegations. You used to see me walk into the cell and out again. People could allege anything. Now they can't.

(CO 8)

Even when referring to just the cameras in the 'public areas' the cameras were thought to provide a useful verifiable record.

We are covering ourselves. I have been through a Disciplinary Board and had the cameras been there I wouldn't have. It makes life easier when dealing with officers. It makes it easier to show the behaviour of detainees. We just don't get complaints now. We don't treat them differently, but the cameras have stopped it [complaints] happening. It's a major bonus.

(CO 9)

But the cameras also apparently had an impact on officers' behaviour, although they were quick to point out that most of the changes related specifically to how they addressed detainees and each other. They insisted that previous styles of policing, when undue force might have been used on detainees, had in most respects long since been abandoned.

Most are very professional. I have never seen abuse of prisoners in my ten years. No one is going to risk losing a £30,000 job for that.

(CO 1)

Suspects, as will be seen, take a somewhat different view. Officers were also aware that their investigating colleagues were affected by the presence of the cameras.

It hasn't affected my role as a CO. It impacts on the way investigators work and on the prisoner's ability to give information confidentially. We would have to take them out of the cell and it would be on record showing this. And a clever barrister could work out who informed if he isn't charged.

(CO 3)

As far as the 'quick word' goes, they can't go and do that anymore. The CID are the worst at that.

(CO 4)

Monitoring

The cameras enabled staff to keep an extra eye on those detainees who were thought to be at risk. These ranged from the drunk, the addicted, the mentally disordered and the many juveniles who passed through the cells, as well as those who were distressed by their predicament. According to custody suite staff, the cameras also had the effect of ensuring that staff took extra care. They acknowledged that the cameras would expose failure to abide by procedures.

... to go back to the care aspect. You get your drunk brought in. In the past they got put in the cell, but now they ensure they are in the correct position etc.

(CO 6)

The only impact is in terms of gaolers. Drunks have to be visited and roused. That must be seen to be done properly.

(CO 1)

With the mentally disordered the cameras were thought to be an even greater help because they enabled staff to monitor unpredictable behaviour. In these cases it was the sense of an extra eye being available which was most welcome.

It's a helpful aid. For instance, we had two people in yesterday, one who had been sectioned and we put him on the single screen. Then we had another one in who was mentally ill and I could put him on the screen ... They are a protection for the prisoner and for us.

(CO 9)

Sometimes there are instances when the FME has advised that a detainee does not need more frequent checks, yet the advice appears at odds with the detainee's behaviour. In those circumstances officers may always choose to check a cell more frequently, but when the custody suite is busy – and often lacking a gaoler – they may not be able to leave the booking desk. The camera, if monitored, can then alert them to changed circumstances.

It assists me. I can seen the banging going on, can see who it is, so I don't have to go down every ten seconds. I can make sure they're not harming themselves.

(CO 7)

Officers can also use the cameras to assess beforehand how to handle various situations in the cells.

I am shield-trained, so set techniques are used for cell relocations. If I have to lead that then I have to make a risk assessment and the CCTV is very useful because you can observe beforehand.

(CO 5)

The cameras can be useful in detecting contraband that has been missed during searches.

They have shown themselves to be useful already. During searches lighters have been missed and the cameras pick up the flash very quickly. Sometimes the p/ds [detainees] are very surprised to know this. If the cameras are there you might as well go the whole hog and video everything. It's a human rights issue and it needs to be tested in the courts – I'm sure it will be at some stage.

(CO 5)

Some don't like it. Some don't notice it at all. With some it's because they can be seen doing certain things they don't want us to see. Once a guy set a fire off. Another had heroin and got high on it. That was poor searching.

(CO 7)

But the cameras can also be used for purposes not publicly spoken about; the detection of criminal behaviour within the cells which can then lead to further charges, such as criminal damage of the cell. However, as we shall see in the next chapter, it was by no means always the case that detainees were aware of cameras in the cells. Using evidence from CCTV under these circumstances might appear to raise questions about fair play.

Some of them know the cameras are in the cells. Some people I allow to have pens and I explain that if they mark the walls they can be charged with criminal damage. Prior to the cameras you didn't always know what was going on.

(CO 11)

At the same time officers were becoming accustomed to the cell cameras, they were encouraged to note incidents they had observed on-screen in a custody log book. From our examination of the post-installation records we knew that the cell cameras had been cited in the custody records 82 times. Of these instances, 70 related to officers' observation of overall behaviour and six dealt with actions within the cells which could have been construed as evidence of offences being committed. By way of contrast, the log book listed 22 incidents, three of which related to the same detainee. Ten of the incidents were entered in the month following the installation of the cameras and, after that, it was almost as if the book had been forgotten.

Two potentially dangerous events were noted; one when a detainee tied a cord around his neck and the other when a detainee set fire to a cell and action was immediately taken in both instances. On another occasion the cameras were used during the removal of a 'violent' detainee from his cell so that officers could plan their cell relocation strategy. Some of the incidents were attempts to cover the camera lens and a few of the entries referred to detainees' concerns about being observed when on the toilet. It is clear, however, that some of the incidents recorded in that book – such as setting fire to a cell – could have been avoided had the initial rub-down search been conducted more thoroughly.

The right system?

The cell cameras, insofar as the officers are concerned, have two paramount functions: providing an extra means of keeping detainees safe while in custody and providing a record of events within the whole of the custody suite. Of prime importance is the officers' duty of care towards detainees. As we have just shown, the cameras facilitate the more frequent monitoring of vulnerable detainees as well as those who are extremely volatile or disturbed. They offer an extra eye to busy officers, with a welcome addition being that they also enable officers to watch out for the safety of colleagues.

A verifiable record is of benefit to both detainees and officers but, as we have already shown, the officers believe it is their *professional* safety which is most guaranteed by the cameras. The extra verification made possible by the cell cameras is seen as a bonus. This had also been expected by officers interviewed earlier.

> [I am] safer from complaints, but not physically. People will attack you, no matter what.
>
> (CO 9)

> Not from physical attack, but from allegations.
>
> (CO 11)

They anticipate that having a taped record will aid their defence, especially when faced with having to answer why they might not have been constantly viewing the monitors. The tapes will show how busy the custody suite was at any given moment, who was present, what was happening, how often cells were visited and checked. In short, they will verify the officers' written records. They will also rebut allegations such as failure to follow procedures as set out in PACE; excessive force having been used, and inappropriate contact with detainees.

It is the tapes which provide the evidence and security so essential, in their different ways, to both detainees and officers. Deciding which recording system should be installed was an initial difficulty for those responsible for planning the Kilburn scheme. When the possibility of cell cameras was first mooted there had been talk about installing a 'closed' system, whereby the cells would be continuously recorded but tapes would only be reviewed should an event need further explanation. (In the event, as previously discussed, an 'open' system was adopted.) We wanted to discuss both the potential and actual schemes with every group of interviewees, to see if there were differences of opinion as to the relative merits of each.

The first officers we interviewed were split fairly evenly regarding the merits of both systems. They appreciated the greater privacy possible with the 'closed' system but were also concerned that safety might be sacrificed as a consequence.

The [open] system may have been useful in seeing those who are suspects, but the [closed] one wouldn't help prevent deaths in custody through illness or drunkenness. So the [closed] system defeats the object of monitoring for protection.

(pre G 4)

The second group, having had direct experience of the 'open' system, largely favoured it. While again conceding that privacy was lost, they thought it preferable to have a means of monitoring detainees, with one saying 'if the cameras are there for the safety of the prisoner then you *must* monitor them' (CO 5). One officer encapsulated two areas of concern: being able to monitor immediately and the decision-making needed to identify those in need of monitoring.

The system we have [now] is okay because even though you're not actively watching it, you *can* monitor it if someone is identified as vulnerable. But you might not always identify them and the camera can help. You can catch a movement out of the corner of your eye.

(CO 6)

This question of prior identification is important because it relates to a recommendation by the PCA that 'CCTV coverage of custody suites should be expanded to include one or two observation cells for particularly vulnerable detainees' (PCA 1999: 12 and 17). Officers are not medically trained and rely heavily on their own instincts as to a person's state of mind and the information provided by detainees when

Form 57M is being completed at the booking-in stage (a risk assessment pro forma). Were it the case that Kilburn had followed the PCA recommendation and installed cameras in, say, two of its seventeen cells, officers would undoubtedly be faced with having to assess the competing needs of prisoners. At Kilburn it is not uncommon for most if not all of the cells to be busy. Under the PCA scheme staff would be faced with the possibility that three or four prisoners might be thought vulnerable and that there would be insufficient monitored cells in which to place them.

This responsibility alarmed the custody officers at Kilburn, not because they are unaccustomed to making such decisions but, perhaps ironically, because the presence of the cameras made them personally feel more vulnerable to accusations of negligence or misbehaviour. Officers would not always be able to answer 'why that suspect rather than another in a videoed cell?' when there might have been competing claims as to who should be placed in available cells.

> It's impossible to decide who is high-risk. It's not infallible, using the questions we have to ask. If you prioritise you risk criticism if you make the wrong choice.
>
> (CO 12)

> The argument is that those prisoners you are concerned about you would put them in a camera cell, but you don't always get it right – and their behaviour can change quite quickly.
>
> (CO 5)

> There's not much point in not covering every possibility. If I decided to put someone in a cell without a camera and he alleged he was assaulted it would be up to me as to why. It's all or nothing.
>
> (G 3)

As has been noted in other contexts, one of the unintended consequences of installing 'security equipment' may be to increase feelings of insecurity, the presence of such equipment being a visible reminder of the possibility of victimisation. Thus, although police officers were generally in favour of the installation of cameras, they worried that the risks they faced with regard to allegations of negligence – particularly if only a limited number of cells were subject to electronic surveillance – would be increased.

Caring for all

What is perhaps not fully apparent from the above is the range of people passing through the cells at Kilburn police station. As we illustrated in Chapter 3, there are some very distinct groups which, in terms of surveillance, are watched like any others, but whose level of care within the station does mark them as being in a different category. Juveniles and others needing the presence of an appropriate adult present particular responsibilities for the police. Following the introduction of PACE, there are stringent rules governing such detainees' detention and their strict application frequently means that juveniles, in particular, are held for considerably longer periods than is the case for a co-accused aged 17 and above. Parents are often unable or unwilling to come to the station to support their child and none of the official procedures can begin until a parental substitute – sometimes a relative, but more often an appropriate adult – arrives. Some of the juveniles are very young indeed and often there are more juveniles in the station than there are detention rooms for them, so some inevitably end up in the cells.

> With appropriate adults we need to re-write the [PACE] *Codes of Practice*. We need professional appropriate adults employed by the police. It is a nonsense to drag in a mini-cab driver from across the street, who might not even have very good English. The Social Services can't cope.
>
> (CO 3)

> At the moment we are doing as much as we possibly can. Sometimes it's difficult – you want to do things right away but can't. Juveniles are a prime example.
>
> (CO 7)

> The appropriate adult system is shambolic. Why can't we have ... as a paid appropriate adult whom we contact at any time without going through Social Services? He should be a Brent employee, but paid by us.
>
> (CO 8)

At the other end of the scale are the number of immigration and asylum detainees held on behalf of HM Immigration Service until arrangements can be made for their deportation or removal to an asylum centre.

> We shouldn't be having immigration cases. To lock them up for three days – the shower facilities are awful, there are no towels, apart from paper ones.
>
> (CO 4)

These detainees can be held for extremely long periods. Some have experienced imprisonment in their own countries and are very fearful of what lies ahead. It is not uncommon for some to remain in the care of the police for periods of up to four days. The cells have no running water, reading material is not available and they have little option but to sit their time out. For the police their detention is an extra burden, especially as it is not always easy to get interpreters and staff have to do their best to understand what the detainee's needs might be. The cameras assist in monitoring, especially as some of these might be regarded as particularly vulnerable but, correspondingly, the cameras also provide a cumulative level of surveillance which could add to the distress of already distressed detainees.

Conclusions

As a result of increasing concerns about the safety of suspects in custody, police forces are beginning to introduce cameras into custody suites. With the exception of Kilburn, however, forces are only installing cameras in a limited number of cells for the surveillance of detainees believed to be at particular risk. The Kilburn experiment is the first to involve continuous 24-hour surveillance of all its detainees. It also, simultaneously and necessarily, involves almost continuous surveillance of its custody staff. In this chapter we explored custody officers' perceptions and experiences of the introduction and operation of cameras. In general, what we found was:

- officers are generally accepting of the cameras;
- they believe the cameras have had a significant impact on both detainees and officers;
- they regret their own loss of privacy, but are prepared to accept it should the cameras prove to be valuable to their work;
- they are also concerned about detainees' loss of privacy;
- officers feel better protected against false allegations but do not generally feel that the presence of cameras makes them physically safer;
- a perhaps unintended consequence of the cameras is that police officers, despite feeling less vulnerable to false allegations, are concerned that criticism will be considerably increased should something bad happen;
- officers generally favour cameras in all cells, not just in selected 'vulnerable' cells.

In talking to these officers it was clear that they felt the cameras would remain part of their working lives, both in the booking area and the cells. Indeed, some clearly felt that this experiment deserved to be extended.

It should be extended to every custody suite, with cameras in every cell. They will get to the stage where they can't afford *not* to have it. You could *save* hundreds of thousands of pounds just by having it, even if it costs thousands to install.

(CO 6)

Everyone should [have them] – the full thing we have now. You can balance the cost against the civil claims.

(CO 8)

You've improved the way people are looked after. It should be elsewhere. I feel vulnerable to complaints. It's for our protection, too. If you go to places without cameras you feel vulnerable. I want the camera to show what I have done. You need the proof on the camera.

(CO 9)

Beyond that, they generally welcomed the additional professional security which the cameras conferred and hoped that other police stations would similarly benefit from CCTV. While some were concerned about the broader implications of the cameras and reflected on possible infringements of human rights, they assumed that the overriding need for protection would be recognised should a challenge reach the courts.

But what also emerged was almost a sense of resignation; that, at some stage, these tapes *would* be produced in court and they would be asked to account for why they had failed to notice something on the monitors. They had little hope that they would be supported by a management which had insisted upon having cameras in the cells, but had not provided the means by which they could be consistently monitored.

If something goes wrong the camera can make you more vulnerable. It will only be a matter of time before something happens, it goes to court and they'll say 'why weren't you watching it?' It's still me in the dock – but I have the Protocol!

(CO 6)

Officers assumed that they might then be held to account for perceived failures to monitor detainees adequately, irrespective of how busy they may have been at the time. Yet they did not raise the possibility that tapes played in court would actually provide proof of professional misconduct, such as mistreatment of detainees by other officers, if not themselves. (As we have already noted, officers generally affirmed a belief in their own – and colleagues' – professionalism.) In other jurisdictions tapes emerging into the public domain have had a devastating impact, most notably in Canada, where 'a video recording [of events within a women's prison] intended to protect staff from false accusations became the vehicle for exposing those staff [and] shocking the public' (M. Shaw 1999).

Nonetheless, overall the views expressed by custody staff were generally very positive. Though they retained some reservations or concerns about the cameras, such reservations were almost always outweighed by the perceived benefits of the system. In the next chapter we move on to consider the views and experiences of the main group being watched; the detainees. How do they experience the cameras? What is the impact of the experiment on their privacy? Do they feel safer and, if so, why? How do they balance the issues of protection and privacy?

Notes

1   The notation on the quotes from interviews will indicate when it was conducted. Those conducted prior to the installation are labelled 'pre CO' (custody officer) or 'pre G' (gaoler); those conducted after installation merely 'CO' or 'G'.
2   The PCA Report *Deaths in Police Custody: the risks reduced* made a number of recommendations specific to the introduction of in-cell CCTV.
3   The role of FMEs (forensic medical examiners), lay visitors, appropriate adults and solicitors is explained in Chapter 6.
4   Though the number of women strip-searched is low numerically compared with men, nonetheless approximately 7 per cent of all female detainees are strip-searched.
5   The question of whether strip searching is a breach of the *Codes of Practice* is most likely to be tested in the courts.

Chapter 5

The view from the cells

Introduction

In this chapter we consider the views of the detainees themselves. As those most directly affected by the installation of cameras in the cells they occupy a unique position as both subjects of, and commentators on, the scheme. How did they experience being watched continuously? What are their views on the questions of 'privacy' and 'protection'? Did they feel that the introduction of cameras had had any impact on their own, or anyone else's, behaviour?

As with the officers, the interviews were conducted in two stages: initially when only the booking area and cell corridors were subject to CCTV cover and then, later, when cameras had been installed in the cells and were working. Obviously, all the detainees interviewed were able to comment on the experience of the cameras in the booking area, whereas only the second interview group had direct experience of the cell cameras. The first group were asked to imagine what introducing cameras would be like and, as we shall show, much of what they had to say anticipated what was later said by those that had direct experience of being watched in their cells.

Although we made no attempt to pre-select a sample of detainees, there was nevertheless an element of selection amongst those whom we eventually interviewed. We were dependent upon individual custody officers for permission to enter each cell. Any detainee incapacitated through alcohol or drugs was immediately ruled out, as were those needing an appropriate adult or with insufficient command of English. We also had to accept the judgement of the police if they said that a detainee's behaviour was liable to be unpredictable and they should not be interviewed.

Almost all the interviews took place in the cells themselves, which meant that the second group of interviewees were being visually recorded by the cameras as they were interviewed (as has already been emphasised, the cell cameras have no audio link). Generally, the cell door would remain closed, but sometimes the wicket (a metal slot in the door) would be left open. All interviewees had the independent nature of the research explained to them, were told that their comments would not be relayed to the police and that the reason for their being in the cells was not to be discussed[1].

The samples

Pre-installation

Twenty-eight detainees were interviewed prior to the cameras being installed in the cells. All but two were men. Of the male detainees, ten were (again self-defined) white, fourteen were black and two were Asian. Of all those describing themselves as white, five were from either Eire or Ulster. The two female detainees were both white. The detainees' ages ranged from 17 to 51, with the largest group being between 21 and 30. The offences they were accused of, broadly categorised, included theft (3), robbery (2), drugs (6), violence (7) and sexual offences (2). Four were immigration detainees and four were wanted on a warrant. The majority had been in the cells for between six and eighteen hours and seven had been detained for over 24 hours. Nineteen had previously been in a police cell and, of these, eleven had been held at Kilburn.

Post-installation

A further 45 detainees were interviewed once the cameras had been installed in the cells, of whom seven were women. In total, 24 were self-defined as white (with six being from Eire or Ulster), seventeen as black and four as Asian. (Of the women, one was black and the others white). Their ages ranged from 17 to 55, with the majority being between the ages of 21 and 30, closely followed by those aged between 31 and 40. Their alleged offences included theft (12), drugs (10), violence (6), burglary (5) and sexual offences (3). Five were immigration detainees and others, charged with specific offences, were also facing deportation. Nineteen had been in the cells for less than six hours, whereas seven had already been detained for more than 24 hours. Thirty had spent time in police cells prior to this arrest and nineteen had previously been in Kilburn.

As we have already implied, much of what the first set of interviewees had to say about the use of cameras in the custody suite matched, very closely, what was said by those in the second group with direct experience of in-cell cameras. Consequently, in most of what follows the respondents are treated as a single sample. An overview of the respondents is provided in Table 5.1 below.

Table 5.1 Demographic characteristics of the overall interview sample

	White	Black	Asian	Total
Male	28	30	6	64
Female	8	1	–	9
Total	36	31	6	73

A core of common questions was asked of both interview groups. The only significant differences in the interviews concerned the addition to the second schedule of questions about the experience of the installed cell cameras. It is primarily in relation to these questions that we focus only on responses from the second group of respondents.

No juveniles were interviewed. In order to do this an appropriate adult would have had to be present – assuming it would have been appropriate to interview juveniles under such conditions at all. Appropriate adults are not readily available and the few on call have many demands made on their time. Consequently, we are unable to present the juveniles' perspectives, and any comments we later make relating to them are general conclusions based on our observations and discussions with those responsible for their care.

Have the cells changed?

Police cells are not comfortable places and those at Kilburn police station are no exception. They suffer from extremes of temperature and the ventilation is poor. The cells are off two corridors and those at the end of each corridor feel – and are – relatively remote from the booking desk. Almost every cell surface is tiled. In each cell the wall furthest away from the door has a narrow wooden-topped bench running along its length, above which is a window composed of small panes of thick, opaque glass.[2] The window has a sill and, following the installation of the cameras, some detainees have climbed onto it while attempting to cover the camera lens with either food or toilet paper. A thin mattress is

Plate 3 View of cell, with triangular camera lens visible in top corner of cell. The toilet is on the wall to the left of the door (photo courtesy of Héloïse Hayman)

supplied, along with a blanket and small pillow. Many find it (marginally) more comfortable to lie down because the bench is too wide to allow detainees to rest their backs against the wall when in a sitting position. Many detainees are reluctant either to sit or lie because they feel uncomfortable about the level of cleanliness, even though the cells are regularly cleaned. The toilets have no separate seat and the top surfaces are badly discoloured. They have no lids and the cells sometimes smell fetid. Toilet paper is provided upon request, but in limited amounts because of fears that a detainee will attempt to block the system. There is no hand basin and drinking water has to be requested.

Detainees are physically observed by the police in four ways: by opening the cell door and checking them inside the cell; by checking them through the raised 'wicket'; through the door 'spy-hole'; or through the spy-hole in the side of the cell, which allows staff to see the toilet area. The installation of the cell cameras provided a fifth means.

During the second stage of the fieldwork anyone walking into a cell at Kilburn might not have immediately realised that they were being filmed and it is conceivable that someone spending a number of hours in a cell could have remained unaware of the cameras. The only visible change

Plate 4 Toilet, as seen by the camera and viewed by detainees from the bench (photo courtesy of Héloïse Hayman)

was the addition of a discreet dark screen, protecting the lens, some distance above where the detainee sits or lies. Cells contained no sign indicating that there was a camera, let alone that it surveyed the entire area. Illustrating the relative invisibility of the camera, some detainees did not realise that they were being observed until the research interview and some of these were most upset at discovering the cameras in this manner.

The interviews with detainees covered their experience of arrival at the police station, their treatment in custody and their views of the entire CCTV system and its possible impact. They were also asked to comment on how others visiting the station might respond to the CCTV and these views are reported in the following chapter, which focuses primarily on the views of solicitors, doctors, lay visitors and appropriate adults.

Arrival at the station

Understandably, detainees were not happy to be in their present situation. However, in the main they acknowledged that their treatment had been reasonable, if often slow.

> I was very impressed and I was surprised at the professional, efficient and polite way I was treated. But I don't think it should have taken ten hours to complete. [I got] only one cup of tea. I asked but they changed shifts. It's obvious that they've taken PACE to heart.
>
> (p/d 30)

By no means all detainees were so polite or restrained in their comments. A number complained about the length of time it took to be allowed to telephone and to get to see their solicitors. Particular frustration was caused by police officers' explanations that they were 'too busy' to attend to them.

> They could be faster. I wanted to make a phone call and it took a couple of hours. I had to ask them a few times and it was always 'too busy, too busy'. The solicitor, too.
>
> (p/d 33)

> I am getting extradited. I haven't been allowed to see my girlfriend and son and they haven't seen me before I go. They [police] say they're too busy! This morning they were talking about football!
>
> (p/d 34)

Others complained about the physical surroundings of the station and the way their needs were attended to.

> I was brought in for questioning and had to spend the whole night here. I can understand that it is not possible to act that quickly, but I

have lost a whole day of work. The solicitor did not want to appear until this morning for interview. It left me all night not knowing where I stood – he could have put me at ease. His advice was 'don't sign anything'. I had just got off to sleep and was woken up to see the FME. I was very dazed. I didn't understand if it was for my benefit or the police's. When you are in a place like this you think that everybody is together. It would have been nice to have been told that the doctor was impartial. My parents rang and the sergeant told them that a visit wasn't worth it. That should have been my decision.

(pre p/d 27)

The food I don't like at all. I had to ask for more blankets. They should see to the heating. It's *very* cold.

(p/d 38)

If I stayed in here I would probably die of hunger – the food sucks.
(p/d 29)

I asked for toilet paper – I have used the toilet three times – and it has not been provided.

(p/d 12)

But generally there were few complaints about other things. They disliked the delays and what they saw as procrastination over dealing with their requests. There were, however, no serious allegations that officers had failed to do their job 'by the book'. Rather, detainees accepted, albeit reluctantly in some cases, that officers had a different perspective about what was important and how long procedures should take. Predictably, time passed exceedingly slowly in the cells.

In what follows we have divided the discussion into two main parts. First, we consider detainees' views and experiences of the cameras in the 'booking area' (the reception area and cell corridors) of the custody suite. Subsequently, we consider their views and experiences of the in-cell cameras.

The cameras in the booking area

Noticing the cameras

As previously explained, the cameras in the booking area had been operating for some time before the fieldwork began so it was inevitable that all the officers we interviewed knew there was CCTV at Kilburn. This was not the case for the detainees, although, on average, almost half of them had previously been held at Kilburn. Two-thirds either already knew or quickly realised that CCTV was operating in the custody suite. Of those that did not, one possible explanation might be that that some were drunk upon arrival or were simply too distressed to observe their surroundings fully.

> I was unconscious and unable to see when brought in here.
>
> (pre p/d 15)

> When you're arrested you can't really think about the camera. You feel angry and annoyed.
>
> (p/d 20)

The visibility of the monitor had alerted most detainees to the presence of CCTV.

> I noticed the monitor first and then concluded there must be cameras and eventually I saw the cameras in the custody areas – but I had to look for them.
>
> (pre p/d 12)

However, few realised the extent of the cameras' coverage (the cameras themselves went relatively unnoticed), often because they spent little or no time in other parts of the booking area where cameras were installed. In other words, unless a detainee had the opportunity to see the full extent of camera coverage of the custody suite, they were unlikely to be aware of it.

In the booking area there are signs alerting detainees to the presence of CCTV (see Figure 5.1).

As is clear, the notice simply talks about the presence of cameras in the custody suite. It makes no reference to particular areas of the custody suite and, more particularly, does not refer specifically to cameras in the cells. It also presupposes that detainees can read, and there is no visual clue that the sign relates to CCTV. The cells contain no notices at all. Of the 73 detainees interviewed, less than one-third (22) had noticed or read the signs alerting them to the presence of the cameras. Again, their state upon reception might be a partial explanation, but also of possible significance is the known number of offenders/those received into prison

Figure 5.1 Notice about CCTV displayed in the booking area at Kilburn

Kilburn Police Station
Brent Borough
ATTENTION
Notice to all persons in
Police detention at Kilburn Police Station

CCTV has been installed throughout the custody suite to
enhance your care whilst in detention.
At all times, unless otherwise stated, your detention will be
monitored and recorded by CCTV.
Any person seen to be damaging Police property whilst in
detention will be liable to prosecution.

who are illiterate. The latest figures show that 50 per cent of those received into prison have poor reading skills and 81 per cent have writing skills lower than the average for an 11-year-old. As police cells are often the gateway to prison, there is no reason to believe that the figures for those detained at Kilburn differ greatly (DfEE 2001). What is clear is that few efforts were made by the police at this stage to warn detainees of the general presence of cameras.

Changing behaviour?

The very fact of the interview meant that all detainees immediately became aware of the CCTV. Consequently, when asked whether the cameras affected their behaviour, some were answering having had relatively little time to consider the possibility. It would appear that this had relatively little impact on their assessments of their own behaviour – the views of those that were already aware of the cameras differed little from those that first became aware of their presence during the course of the research interview. Of all those interviewed, very few conceded the possibility that the cameras could have an impact on how they behaved at the station, although one remarked that had he known he was being filmed he would not have shouted. A few thought that the fact of being in a police station, rather than actually being filmed, occasioned restraint and some detainees expressed the view that the existence of the cameras provided reinforcement to the 'rules' that they felt currently applied in the custody suite.

> You're in a police station. You've got to be pretty well behaved.
>
> (p/d 5)

> I'm not likely to cause trouble – and seeing the cameras would put me off.
>
> (pre p/d 23).

These detainees expressed the view that their behaviour was governed not primarily by the cameras but by broader perceptions of the nature of authority in the police station and the custody suite. This is a reflection of what Tyler (1990: 170) summarises in his discussion of the psychology of legitimacy, where he suggests that 'people generally feel that existing legal authorities are legitimate, and this legitimacy promotes compliance with the law'. It would appear that the majority of the detainees perceived the authority of the police within the custody suite to be legitimate, understood the basic 'rules' of behaviour governing the custody suite, and did not seek to disturb it. They did not appear to see the cameras as being especially important in the maintenance of order.

> You're gonna behave how you're gonna behave. Cameras won't make any difference.
>
> (pre p/d 11)

Almost half the respondents, however, wanted to emphasise that their behaving 'as normal' was not contingent upon their being held at a police station. By implication, being 'as normal' meant being 'well behaved'.

> Because I believe I behave the same way all the time.
>
> (p/d 27)

> Usually this is me. How I treat myself. Under control.
>
> (p/d 35)

For a few their familiarity with CCTV in other contexts had influenced them.

> I was working in a restaurant – there are cameras all the time.
>
> (p/d 31)

> I work with bloody cameras all the time at work. You don't do a misdemeanour in front of the cameras!
>
> (p/d 32)

Detainees' views of other detainees

As far as the behaviour of their fellow detainees was concerned, most of those interviewed believed that a small minority, because of particular personal characteristics, or intoxication, was likely to cause trouble. But, having already explained that the cameras had no impact on their own behaviour – which they overwhelmingly described as remaining 'normal' – the majority of interviewees then assumed that the cameras *would* have an impact on other detainees. They appeared to be saying that other detainees' violence or aggression would be modified once they knew they were being videoed. The distinction to be made here is that detainees did not apply this same logic to themselves, because they did not see their own behaviour as being in need of modification. They found it easier to imagine the misconduct of others, almost as if those they were visualising were more representative of the average detainee than themselves.

> They might misbehave, but would stop when they see the camera.
>
> (pre p/d 28)

> Some of them, it must. They would behave a lot better. They could go the other way – they could put on a show.
>
> (p/d 23)

> Any troublemakers – it should give them second thoughts.
>
> (pre p/d 17)

> They might not be so aggressive towards officers, so violent, if they know they are being monitored every minute.
>
> (p/d 42)

Occasionally, some suggested that the cameras might provoke a reaction or be used to a detainee's advantage.

> Some blokes are arseholes. They will try and act up in front of the cameras. Like on the TV news, when you see people acting up behind interviewers.
>
> (p/d 2)

> They might try and make a sly little comment and try to get the Old Bill to react to it.
>
> (p/d 18)

Detainees' views of the police

By contrast with their own perceived imperviousness or indifference to the cameras, when asked if they thought the police's behaviour might be changed by the cameras in the booking area and corridors, two-thirds of interviewees thought it highly likely that it would. Some, however, suggested that once officers became accustomed to the cameras they would soon become oblivious to them.

> They don't even notice it's there after a while. There are so many cameras wherever you go these days.
>
> (p/d 4)

But many more referred to expected changes in the physical treatment of detainees and there was considerable unanimity of thought between pre- and post-installation interviewees. They often based this quite specifically on what they had heard about the police, rather than what they had themselves experienced.

> In terms of following procedures that may have in the past been skipped. One hears horror stories from the past when prisoners have been abused. It has to be a deterrent if there is a camera.
>
> (p/d 30)

> It stops people from getting hidings, from being fitted up. Years ago, when they didn't have the cameras, British justice didn't have a good reputation. If they had had the cameras then the mistakes made would not have been enforced.
>
> (p/d 16)

> They can't get away with what they used to get away with for years. Like they used to be rough with prisoners and now they can't because they're on camera.
>
> (p/d 34)

The cameras were seen as both having an impact on behaviour and providing a record of that behaviour. This dual function was assumed to apply equally to the police and detainees.

> I would imagine they are conscious of the camera and have to act in a certain way because the camera won't lie. It's just as much for their protection as ours. I could say I had been beaten up when I

walked in and it would show up in their defence. And if I *had* been beaten up, it would show up in *my* defence!

(p/d 43)

Most definitely. They have to be careful, they can't do what they want anymore. Obviously it's different from when they didn't have the cameras.

(p/d 17)

They would have to go through the proper procedures, make sure it was right. They couldn't break the law.

(p/d 33)

Changing police behaviour?

Those detainees familiar with Kilburn police station had also noticed a change in the behaviour of the police and, largely, attributed this to the presence of the cameras, rather than a cultural change.

I never thought about it. In a way, it's good to have them out there. The police are on camera all the time. I've been in trouble for a few years now and when you used to get here you would get some backhanders and the like. But not now.

(p/d 34)

It's a very good idea. Last time I was arrested I did not notice them. Now I can see the change in the behaviour of the officers.

(pre p/d 21)

A very good idea. I'd say the staff are more civil now than when I was here in 1994. That could be CCTV or the Macpherson Report, but who knows? They're better.

(pre p/d 17)

Nonetheless, some concerns remained. There were some indications that detainees could have been better informed about the cameras. As one detainee put it, 'it's a good thing if they let people know the cameras are there. When I came here I was distressed and didn't notice the cameras' (p/d 28).

The cameras as evidence

Whilst it should be remembered that interviewees assumed the cameras modified the behaviour of *other* detainees and, by implication, that those detainees would be more in need of a record of their detention than themselves, they supported the use of cameras because of their evidential value. They felt that cameras in the open spaces would ensure that rules and regulations would be more closely adhered to because of the potential taped evidence they would provide.

> It means they have to play it by the book, don't they? If the cameras weren't there, some of them wouldn't be so careful.
>
> (pre p/d 1)

> Because they are being watched – it helps make them stick to procedure and the law. So violence in custody should decrease.
>
> (pre p/d 17)

There was also an assumption that the cameras were not solely for the protection of detainees; that the record would also provide evidence of detainees' misbehaviour and afford extra protection to the police.

> A very good idea, an excellent idea. It protects both sides, the interests of all parties. The police can be seen to be following proper procedures. A detainee can be seen behaving in a proper manner. If there is a flare-up it protects all concerned.
>
> (p/d 21)

> I think it's good. It protects both arrestees and police from false allegations.
>
> (pre p/d 7).

The storage of tapes

There was, however, some scepticism among detainees about the security and integrity of the tapes should they be needed for inquiries and some found it hard to believe that the police could not turn the cameras off if it suited them to do so. This perception of the way in which the system operated could possibly have been altered had more information been provided for the detainees – and had they all been told about the cameras in the first place. Some of their doubts related to what they had heard and read elsewhere.

I don't know why the cameras are there but I should imagine if anything happened – someone was killed – then I'd expect all the tapes to disappear. I can guarantee that if anything happened to me all the tapes would disappear. There have been so many things happening in police cells.

(p/d 26)

It would be harder for them to get away with something if it's on camera. But then you can always lose a video, it's not 100 per cent safe.

(p/d 7)

The detainees' main concern was that the cameras should play an evidential role (assuming the tapes' safe storage) during their time at the station and they generally did not attempt to differentiate between who was in need of the greater protection, themselves or the police.

It could work in favour of both lots, police and suspects. It proves things for the police. It doesn't bother me. They're [cameras] everywhere now, aren't they?

(p/d 18)

What was the consensus?

Overall, detainees were very positive about the presence of the cameras in the booking area and cell corridors. Over three-quarters (58) of those interviewed felt the cameras were a good thing. Not a single interviewee suggested that there should be no cameras at all in this area of the custody suite. The issue of privacy was not raised at this juncture and there appeared to be no concerns about the cameras observing detainees' contact with the police. Indeed, there was a sense that cameras were so much part of the detainees' everyday world, at their work or in public spaces, that their presence in a police station was unremarkable. Given that the booking area gives little sense of being a place where private business may be transacted, perhaps this is unsurprising. Outsiders may always observe what is going on, be they other suspects, solicitors, lay visitors, cleaning staff or anyone else with access to the area. Custody suites are often busy places and the booking process is highly likely to be observed by others.

Cameras in the cells: anticipation and reality

Setting the scene: what did they know about the cell cameras?

As we have seen in relation to CCTV in the 'public' areas of the custody suite it could not be assumed that detainees would be aware of the cameras' presence. By the time they were interviewed in the cells almost two-thirds of the detainees had realised that they were being observed by a camera. Overwhelmingly, this knowledge was based on their own observation, rather than from information supplied by the police. Whereas one detainee had heard outside in the community that there were cameras, not one detainee had actually been told by the police that there was a camera in their cell.

In addition to a general lack of awareness about the cameras, there was also an absence of information about the monitoring of the CCTV system. Only a very few detainees were able to anticipate accurately how the cameras might be monitored, while others guessed, surmising that there had to be a screen somewhere in the building. Although generally assuming that a monitor, if it existed, would be watched by the police, some detainees expressed the view that this should not happen; they wanted a person independent of the police to monitor the screen.

> I would assume it's visually monitored by a visitor, a civilian, for my safety.
>
> (p/d 21)

At that point all those questioned in the second group were told by the researcher where the monitors were sited, how the two screens operated and who viewed them. Without this information they would not have been able to discuss fully the remaining questions which largely related to in-cell cameras.

Monitoring the cameras

Detainees were asked how often they thought they were actually observed on screen by the officers. Over half thought that it was likely to be 'hardly at all' or 'sometimes'. As we have already indicated, generally speaking custody staff are unable to monitor the screens consistently and, consequently, detainees' assumptions in this regard were largely accurate. Indeed, as officers have received official backing for this with the issuing of the Protocols, at the very least this illustrates some of the limitations of the system of proactive protection the cameras were partly brought in to provide.

The detainees did not possess accurate information about the monitoring of cameras. Their scepticism about its likely effectiveness was again reflected in their responses to the question of how long they thought it would take the police to notice, on the monitor, that something had happened to them in their cell. Fewer than a fifth of detainees were confident there would be a speedy response and one cited his own experience of not being observed.

> I would imagine it's more likely to be recording than having someone looking at it, so not very fast at all.
>
> (p/d 8)

> When they physically come to check you – that's how long it would take.
>
> (p/d 42)

> It all depends when they came to see me [to make a physical check]. I don't think they'd notice it on the camera. [He had been smoking and no one had noticed.]
>
> (p/d 34)

A couple of detainees jokingly suggested that they could put the question to the test by being aggressive towards the researcher ('I could attack you and see how long it takes for someone to come!!!') (p/d 16)). As is more fully explained at the end of this chapter, the researcher experienced some delays in being released from the cell and on one occasion, very early in the research period, had waited a good twenty minutes to be let out.[3] While in her case it should have been quite clear that she was banging on the door for some reason, had officers cared to check the monitor, a detainee can quite quickly be labelled a nuisance if they resort to ringing the buzzer too frequently. They may then find themselves left in a cell which has had the buzzer 'isolated' (turned off). Detainees need to be confident that their calls for assistance will be answered irrespective of how individual officers might feel about them and, when the buzzer is isolated – and there is a larger question as to whether it should – they need to know that a change in their physical circumstances will be noticed on the monitors. Some detainees suggested strategies, but these presupposed that they would be in a fit state to implement them.

> I would have to try and make a movement that is not normal so they would notice me.
>
> (p/d 29)

This need for proactive monitoring was highlighted by other interviewees, who hoped that the individual circumstances of the detainees might make the police more attentive to the cameras.

> It shouldn't take them more than a couple of minutes. Knowing my circumstances [drunk] they should be more vigilant.
>
> (p/d 27)

> If I was drunk or on drugs, someone would be watching over me, so that if I was sick they'd get a doctor. If someone was a potential self-harmer, it would be good. If you request to see a doctor or solicitor or something and it is denied, then everything is on camera. Everything is recorded and monitored.
>
> (pre p/d 11)

Some complexities

In completing the scene-setting it is important to explore some of the ambivalence contained in detainees' answers. In interview, detainees were asked questions that had both 'open' and 'closed' elements. It is here that apparent ambivalence emerged. As one example, detainees were asked, 'overall, how do you feel about the camera in the cell?' To the 'closed' section many indicated that the cameras made little difference to how they felt about being in the cells. Yet their responses to the open-ended section of the same question resulted in quite clear distinctions being made between how they, personally, felt about the cameras as record-keepers and guarantors of protection, and how they felt about the cameras as constantly-monitored disseminators of private actions within the cells. This was in marked contrast to how they were able to make a distinction between themselves and other detainees while under the gaze of the booking area cameras. The theoretical situation became a personal one as soon as they visualised *themselves* as subjects of the cell cameras. They were no longer impervious or indifferent to the cameras and saw themselves as part of a wider group exposed to the cameras' gaze.

Four main themes emerged in interviews with detainees. Firstly, there is the issue of privacy and the extent and manner in which the cameras were experienced as being intrusive. What does 'privacy' mean to those detained in police custody and what are its limits? Secondly, we explore the linked issue of protection. Is in-cell CCTV experienced as a form of protection? In what way, and to what extent does this additional form of protection counterbalance any perceived loss of privacy? Thirdly, and related to the issue of protection, we consider the cameras as providers of evidence and verifiers of the record. Finally, we look at the cameras as a means of communication.

Privacy

Concerns about privacy

Detainees, as we shall see, had a number of concerns about privacy. What emerged from interviews was a set of often 'low-level' general concerns about being 'watched'. Some detainees expressed a high level of discomfort occasioned by worries that they *might* be viewed doing something seemingly foolish, or simply being made to look foolish and exposed. For some detainees, what appeared to alarm them most was the fear or anticipation of possible consequences of being monitored more frequently than they assumed – and not knowing whether that was the case.

> You do silly things when you're bored. You think you're on your own. You count the tiles, things like that, so now I'd feel a bit foolish.
>
> (p/d 16)

> It makes me feel nervous, having it look at me. I don't move around the cell otherwise they think I'm out of my head.
>
> (p/d 13)

There was a sense given by many detainees of an ever-present 'other' waiting to see what they might do next.

> When I go to the toilet or when I am sleeping you can be exposed. It's rude. They should *tell* people before they put them in a cell. You can't tell me cops won't watch. We're not stupid.
>
> (p/d 36)

In the quote above, the use of the word 'watch' by the detainee has a particular meaning. The detainee is distinguishing between 'normal' surveillance – an officer checking that they are well – and other less palatable forms of surveillance, where it is supposed officers may be watching for the purposes of titillation or amusement. One of the implications of this distinction is the sense that there is, in principle, no objection by detainees to the presence of cameras, merely concern about how they will be used and what protection exists to ensure that they are used only for the purposes for which they were intended. However, there was one area of surveillance that was more widely perceived and experienced as problematic.

Using the toilet facilities

With the exception of one group of detainees, the concerns about privacy centred around the filming of the toilet area of the cell. Detainees, in general, were very concerned about being filmed on the toilet.

> It's a bit embarrassing using the lavatory. Why is the camera facing that way? People get searched before they come in [for drugs, etc.] so why have it there? It seems a bit strange.
>
> (p/d 6)

> I don't want to go to the toilet. I'm quite happy for people's safety, but I don't know what I would do if I was here all day. [This woman had already been in the cell for three hours and was still there four hours later.]
>
> (p/d 7)

> You'd have no privacy on the lavatory or whatever. You don't want some cop sitting there watching you use the toilet.
>
> (pre p/d 12)

A number of detainees suggested ways in which cameras could film the whole cell, including the toilet area, while modesty or privacy was being protected (such as with the use of screens). Others suggested precautionary measures they would personally take to ensure that genital areas could not easily be seen.

> Going to the toilet. They can see you and there'd be a lack of privacy. If they screened your body off that would be fine – and then the rest of the time it would be fine.
>
> (pre p/d 6)

> When I go to the toilet I find it difficult. You have to put the toilet paper in front of you [mimes covering the penis] to hide yourself.
>
> (p/d 2)

Though general concerns were expressed about the filming of the toilet area of the cell, detainees expectations about privacy actually appeared to differ fairly markedly according to their cultural backgrounds and personal histories.

Cultural expectations

There was a cultural dimension to the nature of the detainees' explanations of their reservations about being filmed. Kilburn police station, like many police stations, particularly in major urban areas, is situated in a very ethnically diverse area. Electronic surveillance, as practised at Kilburn, carries on regardless of the personal circumstances, ethnic or cultural background of the person in the cell.

> My Muslim culture cannot allow anyone to see someone else go to the toilet. This is the same for Asian culture generally – Hindu, Muslim. The most important thing would be to protect your lower body from view.
>
> (pre p/d 16)

> This balance between privacy and protection is important. Going to the toilet is absolutely a private moment and while people's attitudes might change culturally, it is also about individuals. This is not just about being Muslim, but also Pakistani and Asian. This is a multicultural country and so that needs to be considered.
>
> (pre p/d 16)

Gendered expectations of privacy

The likelihood that expectations and responses would differ between male and female detainees was anticipated by some of the male respondents.

> It might well be an issue for ladies. For gents it doesn't seem nice that someone can see you go to the loo.
>
> (pre p/d 16)

> It's an infringement. The camera being pointed at the toilet does my head in. It would be worse for women. When I had a poo earlier I couldn't go – you remember it's on.
>
> (p/d 2)

> Girls come in here, too, and they menstruate and it's not very nice.
> A toilet is a private place.
>
> (p/d 12)

The interviews with female detainees appeared to confirm that they were much more concerned about the likely intrusiveness of CCTV than the majority of men and, most specifically, with regard to being viewed when using the toilet. This worry about surveillance was not confined to the cameras, however, for they already experienced significant discomfort with the present arrangements where the toilet can be viewed through the wicket in the cell door and spy-hole in the wall.

> It's an invasion of privacy, massively so. It's bad enough that they can just drop that wicket and look in at any time. I'm really conscious of my privacy. Maybe for especially vulnerable people it would be okay, but not for ordinary people. I'd never go to the toilet, I probably wouldn't sleep. It would make me feel really on display and insecure. I'd hate it. As it is, I haven't been able to go to the toilet as I'm worried they'll suddenly decide to look at me through the wicket.
>
> (pre p/d 7)

Yet the cameras, while invading the women's privacy, also afforded protection by way of the recorded evidence which the tapes would contain.

> Maybe women might mind more. They'd feel unnecessarily exposed if they were stripped – but it would also be in their interest if someone does anything indecent, or whatever.
>
> (p/d 22)

Some of the concerns on behalf of women were linked to the question of who might be doing the monitoring, an issue already raised in Chapter 5. This uncertainty, and the possibility that their predicament could be a source of entertainment, reinforced the women's feelings of helplessness.

> The only thing bothering me would be having someone watching you on the toilet. They could be watching you and having a laugh. A woman might find it harder. Are there males watching females in the cells? Or is it females?
>
> (p/d 18)

Privacy and previous experience of custody

Although we did not ask if detainees had served prison sentences in the past, some volunteered this information during their interviews. Those that had been in prison previously appeared to hold no serious reservations about the installation of cameras in cells, and similarly not to be at all concerned about what was filmed. In part, this reflected the earlier point about the mistrust of police officers (and wanting to have a record of events), possibly because of previous experience or what they had heard of mistreatment. However, the absence of concern about this aspect of privacy was also seemingly related to the very different standards of privacy that they became accustomed to in prison. As a consequence, those that had previous experience of custody appeared generally to have fewer qualms about what others might feel to be 'a lack of privacy'.

> Privacy? That's not so important. Once you've been in prison, you realise toilets don't have to be private, though that's not very nice. If it stops police kicking someone about, then going to the toilet doesn't matter so much.
>
> (pre p/d 13)

> Everyone watches you shit and shower in prison, so why does it matter here?
>
> (pre p/d 9)

Police cells, like prison cells, are covered by Crown Immunity, so are exempt from prosecution under Health and Safety legislation. This means that toilets may be placed in what is usually considered to be a living area. The Metropolitan Police have not adopted Prison Service practice of installing a small privacy screen to the side of the toilet. As can be heard in these quotes, and runs through the interviews with detainees generally, being filmed on the toilet was seen to be the most obvious form of intrusion. This is, of course, by no means surprising and reflects a broad set of social mores concerning privacy and bodily functions.

Norbert Elias, in his theory of the civilizing process (Elias 1978, 1982), describes in great detail the changing social mores concerning various bodily functions from the Middle Ages to the twentieth century. He details changing standards of conduct and, as importantly, the progressive cultivation of feelings of shame associated with such bodily functions. Such changing standards and feelings are most obvious in connection with sexual activity and with defecation and urination –

activities now overlaid with complex expectations and assumptions about privacy and modesty. The social arrangements governing defecation for most people in the West now ensure that these expectations of privacy and modesty are relatively easy to maintain. There are, of course, exceptions. Small children are, at least partially, exempt from these expectations. Few exceptions are made for adults. One exception, however, is the very different status occupied by inmates in prisons. The absence until relatively recently of integral sanitation in prison cells, and the fact that prisons were often overcrowded and cells were shared, meant that such bodily functions could not be done 'unobserved' by others. As it was described by the Chief Inspector of Prisons in 1984,

> [overcrowding] results in most of these inmates having to use their pots in the presence of one or two other inmates in the confines of a small cell. When the time for slopping out comes the prisoners queue up with their pots for the few toilets on the landing. The stench of urine and excrement pervades the prison.
>
> (Stern 1989: 81)[4]

One consequence of experiencing life under such conditions, it would appear from the accounts of detainees interviewed at Kilburn, is a somewhat transformed set of expectations about privacy, modesty and bodily functions (certainly among male detainees). What is perhaps most remarkable, however, about detainees' observations on the subject of privacy is the almost complete absence of any concerns other than those regarding filming the toilet area.

As we outlined above, a small number of detainees said that they had general worries about being watched, particularly if they felt that they would be made to look ridiculous. However, this was expressed by a small minority only. It is possible, of course, that such were the concerns about the filming of the toilet area that other concerns about invasion of privacy were relegated and not discussed. It is also conceivable that many detainees would not have envisaged strip searching being carried out in the cells, so would not have commented on them. Were it the case that the toilet area of the cell was not filmed it is possible that detainees would have discussed other worries and concerns. We cannot rule out this possibility, though it seems to us unlikely that detainees would fail to mention completely other significant concerns about invasion of privacy because of the primary concern about the toilet area.

Protection

Previous experience or fear of mistreatment

Over half those interviewed assumed that the cell cameras would ensure that procedures were carried out properly by the police and that detainees would be treated with greater courtesy. This was true both of those interviewed before the cameras were installed in the cells, and those interviewed subsequently. There was also an assumption that physically abusive behaviour would be lessened but in some cases talk of physical abuse was based on what was thought or believed happened in police custody rather than their own previous experience at Kilburn Station. However, those detainees who claimed that at some stage in the past they had been assaulted by the police, were strongly in favour of the installation of cameras in the cells.

> [CCTV] would make them [the police] monitor their behaviour. No one gets smashed up in the custody office, but in the cells and the van is where I've been roughed up... Cameras really need to be in the vans and the cells.
>
> (pre p/d 9)

> At Paddington Green I was beaten twice a day for three days, from Tuesday to Friday, in 1990. According to the police, I assaulted the police first, which is incorrect. CCTV would have proved my innocence. I know people who have been beaten and who have been killed in the cells. CCTV would show their health or condition at the time of arrival in the cells and so that would be the best way of protecting the health or interests of a suspect.
>
> (pre p/d 3)

> They have to make sure they do things correctly. The way they charge you, talk to you, treat you. They can't be violent or abuse you verbally. [A number of detainees found it hard to believe that the cell cameras were not audio-linked.]
>
> (p/d 33)

Protection of other detainees

As we have previously suggested, detainees tended to divide their fellow arrestees into two groups: a small minority who, like themselves, would tend to be relatively unaffected by the presence of cameras, and a majority whose behaviour might be affected by the cameras. This pattern of assuming that their own behaviour was not typical repeated itself when they were asked how they thought other detainees might behave under the gaze of the cell cameras. While a proportion said that they could not speak for anyone but themselves, half believed that the behaviour of other detainees would be affected by the cameras.

> Not everybody has the same behaviour as me – sit back and relax. It could be a phobia being looked at all the time.
>
> (p/d 13)

Protection is intimately linked to being safe from harm inflicted by others, but two-thirds of detainees assumed that the cameras would be of most benefit to those vulnerable to self-harm or generally at risk. They thought that this was the prime reason for the installation of the cameras, but that problems could sometimes arise.

> The groups I think of are those with mental illness. My wife works with people with mental illness and they had to take the cameras away from the day centre where she works because of the difficulties.
>
> (p/d 21)

> It's a psychological thing – someone can see me and I can't see them. Someone suffering from paranoia could turn quite nasty knowing they're being watched. The positive points? – only for security and health. They ask questions when you arrive so should know the answers [to attempt to predict how detainees will behave].
>
> (p/d 21)

Protection and privacy through limited cell cameras?

At the booking-in stage detainees are asked a series of questions designed to ascertain whether they need an appropriate adult and/or medical attention. An appropriate adult may be required if the detainee has reading problems; a mental handicap; attended a special school; mental health problems or a mental illness. If the detainee is suffering from any medical condition, illness or injury; is receiving treatment and/or medication for any of these; or has ever attempted self-harm, then medical attention may be sought. Knowing that the police ask these questions, and because the same questions are asked of each detainee, some respondents were puzzled by the decision to have cameras in every cell, rather than just a few. They assumed that the police could take sufficient precautions and that they, as a consequence, might be left with a greater degree of privacy.

> It's bad. They should put cameras in cells for people who are dangerous. They can take shoes and belts off. They can take precautions.
>
> (p/d 36)

As we discussed in Chapter 2, the Kilburn experiment was fairly controversial at the time of its introduction. Within New Scotland Yard there was concern, in particular, that the installation of cameras in all of the cells in the custody suite might be found to contravene the Human Rights Act and the right to a 'private life'. There was considerable pressure from some quarters to confine the project to the installation of cameras in a limited number of cells only (in line with general practice elsewhere, with Police Complaints Authority recommendations and as suggested by the respondents mentioned above). Moreover, as we have illustrated in this chapter there are indeed concerns expressed by detainees about intrusiveness, particularly in relation to the filming of the toilet area of the cell. However, as we will shortly show, detainees appeared to be more concerned about having the 'protection' the cameras offered than they were about losing their (limited) right to privacy within the cell.

As is generally the case with rights, a sense of 'balance' has to be achieved. The suggestion of a more limited use of cameras was another attempt to bring balance – by providing protection for the most vulnerable (who could be placed in cells with cameras), whilst protecting the privacy of the rest. We asked detainees their views of such an arrangement. Over two-thirds of respondents thought this a bad idea and, when discussing it, the majority raised the issue of protection.

> Protection. If they had a camera in there [gestures towards next cell] but not in here and that person was being troublesome, all they'd have to do would be to bring that person in here and anything could happen.
>
> (p/d 6)

> If you are having them in cells you should have them in *every* cell. Otherwise, if something goes wrong and it's in the cell without a camera...
>
> (p/d 43)

Detainees emphasised the constant need for vigilance and how this would be compromised were cameras to be confined to a few cells. The majority of detainees interviewed after the cameras had been installed thought it essential that cameras should be in every cell, largely because of the protection afforded and because it removed discretion about cell-placement from the police.

> If you're having a system you can't have 'bolt-holes' or blind spots. It has to be comprehensive.
>
> (p/d 30)

The camera as evidence

Verifying the record

Over half of the detainees thought that the cell cameras would have an impact on the behaviour of the police and assumed this change would not be limited to the police's physical interaction with them. In thinking about the cameras as possible guarantors of protection, detainees made a distinction between the CCTV's capacity to influence behaviour simply by its presence (its deterrent effect), and the evidential value of the cameras' tapes. For some, there was an inherent distrust of the police and this extended to the veracity of the written record. Detainees assumed that the tapes would verify their version of events and that they would be less susceptible to being 'fitted up'.

> From the perspective of being monitored, it modifies behaviour towards correct procedures. If I had a heart condition, under stress, had not told them and suddenly fell on the ground – they would need to show they had [physically] checked [the cell].
>
> (p/d 21)

> [It stops the police] from doing stupid things they tend to do. The camera shows something. When I came in there was something in foil on the floor. They say it dropped from my socks, so when I go to court I will tell them to look at the film on the camera.
>
> (p/d 41)

Local knowledge of untimely deaths in police custody emerged during the interviews and the controversial death of Marlon Downes, in nearby Harlesden police station, was mentioned by some interviewees as an event that could have been more readily explained had cameras been in place at the time.

> In case there are any deaths, so they don't get any blame. So they've got it all on tape. Deaths – someone hanging themselves, the police killing someone. In Harlesden police station someone died and to this day no one knows how he died. No one will ever know if they killed him or he killed himself.
>
> (p/d 6)

> The reason is, they had to [install the cameras] – because of all the rubbish going on, beating people up. People supposedly hanging themselves.
>
> (p/d 26)

Yet detainees clearly understood that the provision of evidence was just as much for the benefit of the police as it was for those held in custody. Over a quarter of detainees suggested that the cameras could be used to disprove allegations against the police – and some suggested that this was the prime reason for having cameras.

> If I wanted to hang myself it would be on camera. It's to back themselves up.
>
> (p/d 18)

> Because of allegations – the police always get the blame. Maybe it's for their benefit. But they couldn't [be seen to] do it just for *their* benefit – they'd have to lie about it!
>
> (p/d 17)

> To keep a check on what people are doing. There are people who commit suicide. They [police] are able to come and see that something is going on. It could protect the police. They can act quickly. It provides evidence of police behaviour.
>
> (p/d 9)

Some detainees also thought that video evidence could be used to support the police in bringing charges against detainees who committed further offences while in the cells.

> It could be for vandalism. To stop people lying about the Old Bill.

To back up what the police say – it's all on camera.

(p/d 18)

Augmenting the record

More specifically, other detainees felt that there was a particular purpose behind the cameras and that this explained why the cameras recorded the toilet area of the cell.

People tend to conceal drugs in their backsides and they have to squat to get them out, so it's perhaps why it's aimed that way [at the lavatory]. In case people try to commit suicide, too. Violent prisoners are less likely to attack the police if there is a camera sitting there.

(p/d 12)

Drugs are a big problem. People smuggle things into cells. I could have brought in a lot of things. The search was pretty lax.

(p/d 21)

In commenting on the search the detainee was highlighting a point raised by custody officers when discussing the potential use of the cameras (although no officer admitted that their searching was anything less than adequate). The cameras became an additional professional aid for the police as they were used to provide evidence of the possession of contraband such as cigarettes, lighters, weapons and drugs which might have been missed during a search, or been secreted internally.

Other detainees suggested that the cameras would be a useful way of recording the injuries they had sustained before reaching the station, not because they wished to complain, but because they felt that they had previously had difficulties in getting medical attention.

If there was a camera, I would make sure the camera saw and recorded whatever damage there was on my body so that it could be seen that I need the doctor.

(pre p/d12)

Approximating privacy – the 'closed' versus the 'open' system

As we have shown in earlier chapters, the CCTV scheme was initially planned to be a 'closed' one (i.e. video recordings of the cells would be made but only watched retrospectively if a particular incident had occurred). In the interviews with custody officers the worth of this option was explored, as it was with detainees. In the main, they were asked the same questions as the custody officers. There was a considerable degree of overlap in replies from the two groups.[5] Although detainees accepted that the 'closed' system would allow for more privacy, over half believed that the competing claims for protection were of much greater importance.

> It would be pointless – what is the point? Prevention is better than a cure. If someone bangs their head and fractures their skull and the police don't know, well, great! It could have been prevented.
>
> (p/d 21)

> It's good that you can refer to it, but if it's not being monitored by the police, how can they monitor your health and well-being? It's a waste of time having cameras if they can't see them at the same time. You need to have them monitored at the time.
>
> (pre p/d 5)

> I don't think that's wise. It's stupid. If something happens they have to check the video. How will they know if someone is sick?
>
> (p/d 38)

> That would be fine when you needed facts, but no good for the person hurting themselves deliberately. It wouldn't bring help.
>
> (p/d 43)

These replies echoed the views of custody officers, although detainees were more likely to question *why* others might be allocated to specific cells while officers more generally wondered *how* they could reach such decisions in the face of competing claims for extra surveillance.

Those who preferred the 'closed' system because of the greater privacy it offered (a relatively small minority), generally spoke of the need to be able to use the toilet without being observed (and this system would certainly lessen the worries about offending cultural mores).

> That [a closed system] would sound better. I've been needing the toilet for a long time now but I don't want to go because of the camera. There's a bell for emergencies and they act on it very quickly.
>
> (p/d 12)

Half said there would be no difference to their *personal* level of safety if the cameras were not monitored. This was partly because being in a police cell did not leave them feeling unsafe in the first place and partly because they were sceptical of the level of monitoring possible with the 'open' system. But others insisted that their safety and that of others would be compromised if the cameras were not monitored regularly.

> Some people who are known to the police might feel safer if there were cameras always being watched.
>
> (p/d 43)

> Someone should be watching you all the time, but there should be privacy.
>
> (pre p/d 24)

The central conundrum captured by this last detainee – how to provide both protection *and* privacy – led other respondents to propose having a cell, or cells, in which particularly vulnerable prisoners might be placed and which would contain cameras.

> It would be good for those who are suicidal or violent. Certain cells should have one system [i.e. open], certain cells the other [closed].
>
> (pre p/d 27)

> It could be useful if someone is suicidal or has seizures, but for someone like me it makes no difference. I would not mind so much if I was asked and could refuse.
>
> (pre p/d 2)

But, as we have already seen in this chapter, most detainees were against the idea of only having a few cells fitted with cameras. In essence, however, this is the road that most forces that have custody suite CCTV have gone down, and is the model that the PCA has proposed. It is not an approach that generally receives the approbation of detainees.

CCTV as a means of communication

As we have already described, there is an ever-present issue of communication within the custody suite. On the one hand, detainees often feel isolated and unable to communicate their needs to custody officers and gaolers. On the other hand, custody suite staff frequently feel beset by a constant bombardment of requests and demands, many of which they feel to be unreasonable and a waste of time. This is a source of sometimes considerable tension within the custody suite.

Perhaps not surprisingly, therefore, some detainees viewed the prospect of the introduction of an 'open system' of CCTV very positively as a potential method of attracting the attention of the gaoler or custody officer when there was no other means of communication. The fact, they assumed, that the police would not be able to switch off the cameras was a source of gratification to those detainees whose call buttons/alarms had been deactivated by busy gaolers. Personal experience of how important this could be occurred during the course of the research. At the conclusion of an interview in a cell (prior to the installation of the cell cameras), the interviewer found the call button was 'isolated' (turned off) and that banging on the door and shouting (to the merriment and accompaniment of other detainees in adjoining cells) only brought assistance after 25 minutes. The police apologies and embarrassment simply reinforced the clear recognition that a detainee in need of medical assistance could easily suffer serious harm or death in that time. As the interviewee in this case stated:

> The buzzer's not working; someone could have killed themselves or something [but with CCTV] They can see you so that's good. The buzzer's not working now so I could just wave at the camera.
>
> (pre p/d 14)

But it was not only prior to the installation of the cell cameras that a researcher had difficulty in being released from the cell and this raises questions about the effectiveness of the Protocol-sanctioned intermittent monitoring. In one instance the researcher discovered that the cell alarm buzzer had been 'isolated'. On the assumption that it would soon be noted that she was standing by the door, rather than sitting interviewing, she waited some minutes before banging on the wicket, as this could be rattled. With no response forthcoming, she resorted to kicking the door, again to no avail. Finally, the interviewee offered to batter the door on her behalf, which he did to great effect, and she was released from the cell some twenty minutes after completing the interview. On another occasion she could not be released because the gaoler had gone to another part of the station, carrying all the cell keys with him. This necessitated a wait of ten minutes, not a difficulty in the circumstances, but raising questions about what might have happened had she or another detainee needed help during that time. By contrast, during another interview the interviewee became increasingly agitated and the researcher decided to terminate the interview, but did not wish to make this clear to the detainee. She suggested that some of his concerns might best be answered by the police themselves and her call was responded to immediately. The officer who arrived quietly talked through the detainee's worries and the interview was not resumed. As a detainee commented:

> The buzzers should help if someone needs urgent medical attention. The police often ignore this at present. What's to say they won't ignore CCTV as well?
>
> (pre p/d 12)

The way forward

Detainees were asked if they had any further comments to make on the use of CCTV in police stations and, of the post-installation interviewees, almost a half suggested that the scheme should be extended to other stations. Some had reservations about how widely it should be extended, but believed that the cameras offered a degree of safety that could not always be matched by the statutory physical checks. They emphasised the evidential role of the cameras and some surmised that they would lead to greater public confidence in the police.

> It would be a good idea in every station. For the safety of the prisoners. It would provide a record. Someone couldn't say they had been hit if they hadn't – it would be on camera.
>
> (p/d 25)

> Other stations should have them. The ones that are troubled, that are used more, with loads of arrests, in a high crime area. In those areas the police tend to keep to the guidelines. Inner London and other major cities. Where there have been deaths in stations.
>
> (p/d 42)

> It depends on the statistics, if they show it helps. There are places outside London which might not need it. I have no problem with the camera. It might help the community trust the police.
>
> (p/d 9)

Conclusion

During these interviews detainees provided very diverse responses to the various questions. They acted as commentators on other people's supposed behaviour, while maintaining that their own position was unique and that they were not representative of the larger group. Yet, in anticipating the behaviour and reactions of others, they also displayed considerable concerns of their own and these largely centred on the twin questions of privacy and protection. Inevitably, their responses were governed by their own particular situations and how long they had been obliged to remain in custody yet, with all this diversity, there were themes common to them all.

Overall, they welcomed the use of cameras in the *booking* area, and believed that:

- their own behaviour was unaffected by the cameras;
- the behaviour of other detainees and the police was changed by the cameras in that they encouraged greater restraint on both 'sides'.

In the *cell* area they believed that:

- their own behaviour was unaffected by the cameras (although this was generally belied by their comments);
- the behaviour of other detainees and the police *was* changed by the cameras;
- the way in which the toilets were filmed was of major concern;
- the cameras were believed to have a valuable evidential role; and
- the cameras were perceived to offer protection both to themselves and to the police.

Privacy only became a real issue of concern when cameras in the cells were considered – and then it was of great importance. There was a sense that the cell cameras had crossed a dividing line, and:

- they felt they should have been forewarned about the cell cameras;
- many were very disturbed by the fact that others could observe them on the toilet;
- some worried about the possibility of cross-gender monitoring of the

cameras, especially when they were using the toilet or being strip-searched.

Their concerns about the cameras were fuelled by the failure of the police to explain how they were monitored and this led detainees to believe that the police had control of when the tapes could be stopped and started. This fed their apprehensions, based largely on hearsay, about how they might be treated while at the station. Detainees were similarly worried about the security of the tapes should an incident happen during their period of detention. These concerns in turn led to the question of public confidence, the enhancing of which was ostensibly the rationale for the entire scheme.

Overall, their wish for protection tended to outweigh their concerns about loss of privacy and most, albeit reluctantly, supported the use of cameras within the cells if it meant that 'one life could be saved'. Overall, detainees were in favour of the use of CCTV within the custody suite.

> Until the cameras were here I've never been treated well by the police at Kilburn. I've been beaten up by ten of them at one stage in the past and also flung into my cell by four of them. Now they are better than any police I have seen anywhere, on account of the cameras ... I [was] assaulted twice here – twice before the cameras went in, and I am amazed at their behaviour now. It is so good. The cameras have made a huge difference – every policeman is well behaved now. So the cameras are a really good thing.
>
> (pre p/d 5)

In the following chapter we examine the perspectives of others charged with the care of these detainees – the solicitors, doctors, lay visitors and appropriate adults. Our concern is what impact the cameras had on their work within the custody suite and the extent to which their views about the operation and purpose of the system match those of police officers and detainees. We also consider the views of detainees and officers towards these outside groups, while continuing to pursue the themes of privacy and protection discussed in this and previous chapters.

Notes

1   In considering individual interviews it should be noted that there was a marked difference in the level and length of some of the interviewee's responses. Understandably, most were concerned with their immediate future and an

interview was yet one more thing they had to contend with. For some, it was a break from the monotony of a lengthy detention, whereas for others it was something to which they somewhat reluctantly agreed. A few were on medication and had difficulty remaining awake. With a number, English was not their first language and their limited proficiency was not always apparent until after the interview had begun. This meant that some of the ideas contained in the interview schedule could not easily be discussed and, on occasion, were perhaps not fully understood in the first place. Interviews conducted prior to the cameras' installation are labelled 'pre p/d'; those conducted after installation merely 'p/d'.

2 See the front cover of the book.

3 At the time she was left with the distinct impression that this was not unconnected to the fact that an officer did not wish her to interview in the cells and that she was being shown who had the final authority within the custody suite. As such it was another illustration (like the examples later in this chapter) of the way in which power and authority can be, and sometimes are, exercised in the custody suite.

4 The European Committee for the Prevention of Torture in its visit to prisons in the UK found no evidence of torture but concluded that 'the cumulative effect' of overcrowding, slopping out, and lack of activity amounted to 'inhuman and degrading treatment' (S. Shaw 1999: 266).

5 It should also be pointed out that some of the detainees had difficulty understanding the concept of 'closed' videoing because of their somewhat limited command of English.

Chapter 6

We're all on camera now

Police custody suites are the centre of a complex network of activity. Not only do they contain officers and detainees, but they constantly receive visits from outside agencies and individuals charged with the care of detainees. PACE comprehensively defines who should have access to detainees and in this chapter we consider the views of these outsiders, particularly in connection with the use of CCTV in the custody suite at Kilburn. At each stage of the fieldwork we have interviewed solicitors, doctors, appropriate adults and lay visitors, exploring many of the issues we also discussed with detainees and officers. In addition, during the course of interviews with police officers and detainees we explored how they viewed others using the custody suite, such as solicitors and forensic medical examiners (FMEs). These responses are also included in this chapter. As with the officers and, generally, the detainees we made no attempt to pre-select our sample. We begin with a brief discussion of the roles of each of these outside groups before moving on to consider their particular views.

Solicitors

When detainees are taken to the custody suite for booking-in, PACE requires that they must be told by the custody officer that they have the right to:

- speak to an independent solicitor free of charge;
- have someone told that they have been arrested; and

- consult the PACE *Codes of Practice* covering police powers and procedures.

As we have already seen – and this chapter will also expand upon – the *Codes of Practice* precisely define how a detainee shall be dealt with, and treated, while in a police custody suite. Section C6 of the *Codes* outlines the right to legal advice. As shown in Chapter 3, slightly under one-half of detainees (45 per cent) requested the services of a solicitor (which is a different percentage from those actually seeing a solicitor, once requested). This is a similar proportion to estimates provided in previous research. In the Home Office study (Bucke and Brown 1997), 40 per cent of detainees requested legal advice. The slightly higher proportion recorded in this study suggests the continuing of an upward trend that has been visible since the introduction of PACE. We did not attempt to discover just how many requests for legal advice translated into telephone or face-to-face consultations, but did note how many times solicitors went into the cells for consultations. Asking to see or speak to a solicitor does not necessarily mean that a detainee will actually see a qualified solicitor, as it is not uncommon for an accredited legal representative or trainee solicitor to attend the station instead.

Custody officers are required to hand detainees a *Notice to Detained Person*, which begins with a statement listing those to whom they have a statutory right to speak or to inform of their detention, as outlined above. Assuming that an individual detainee is able to read, this notice then goes on to clarify how free legal advice is made available. A detainee:

- can speak to a solicitor at the police station at any time, day or night;
- may have access to a solicitor delayed only in exceptional circumstances;
- can talk to a solicitor *in private* [emphasis added] on the telephone and a solicitor may visit him/her at the station;
- may have a solicitor present while being questioned by the police (and that such interviews are only exceptionally carried out prior to the detainee having spoken to a solicitor);
- may change their mind about having a solicitor and is free to request one at any stage of detention.

Section C6.1 of the *Codes* stipulates that detainees may 'at any time consult and communicate privately, whether in person, in writing or by telephone with a solicitor' and it is this right which is of primary relevance to this research. The custody suite at Kilburn does not have a telephone in a private booth and any detainee wishing to speak to a solicitor initially by telephone will have to use the one that is placed opposite the booking desk, where conversations can be overhead by officers. Since the installation of CCTV, the conversations will also be recorded by the booking area cameras which are, as we noted, audio-linked. Should a consultation actually take place at the station there is only one consultation room, so solicitors have been accustomed to seeing clients in their cells, if that appears to be the only option.

Eleven solicitors or accredited legal representatives were interviewed as part of this study. Of these, two were women and all but one were white. Seven were over the age of 35. Six were accredited legal representatives and five were qualified solicitors. Eight had been visiting Kilburn police station for over four years. Interviews were conducted either at the station or in their own offices.

Appropriate adults

As we discussed in Chapter 1, the position of custody officer was created in 1984, at the time PACE came into force. The role of appropriate adult was also created at the same time and such people play an essential part in the day-to-day working of any custody suite. Appropriate adults are required to give support to juveniles and both mentally disordered and mentally handicapped detainees. In short, they are to support any detainees who may be deemed vulnerable. While there is no discretion allowed the police regarding calling appropriate adults for juveniles, as this is mandatory, the decision to call them for other detainees is dependent partly upon the judgement of the officer booking in the detainee. As we already know, detainees do not, will not or cannot, always provide accurate information when questioned for Form 57M (which asks about the detainees' educational history, mental state and past history of self-harm) and it is left to the officer to decide whether they will summon support for the person standing before the booking desk.

An appropriate adult may only act for the detainee if they are not personally involved in the alleged offence (which will sometimes mean that a parent, guardian or sibling may be disbarred). Solicitors may not act as appropriate adults and lay visitors may only fulfil that function when they are not at the station in their capacity as a lay visitor. Persons also thought to be suitable for the work may be a social worker or 'someone who has experience of dealing with mentally disordered or mentally handicapped people but who is not a police officer or employed by the police' (*Codes* C1.7(b)(ii)). Although parents or guardians are usually the first choice of the custody officer, when they are unavailable or refuse to assist, the officer will then summon one of the above or, 'failing either', 'some other responsible adult aged 18 or over who is not a police officer or employed by the police' (*Codes* C1.7(b)(iii)). What is particularly important about the role of appropriate adults is that information disclosed to them by the detainee is not privileged and that it may be revealed to the police. This is not necessarily understood by the detainee and, as Palmer discusses (1996: 7) raises questions about an appropriate adult's ability fully to 'advise and assist' (*Codes* C3.12) a vulnerable detainee.

Relevant to our research (and discussed in Chapter 3) is the length of time it generally takes for an appropriate adult to come to the station. Officers will usually attempt to persuade a parent or family member to attend the station, but it is not uncommon for there to be a refusal. They will then approach others, such as social workers, or those who are on the list of approved appropriate adults. All this can take a considerable amount of time, during which the juvenile, or mentally disordered or handicapped detainee, will have to wait in the detention rooms or cells. Without an appropriate adult being present these detainees may not:

- be interviewed (except in urgent cases);
- provide or sign a written statement;
- be intimately or strip-searched; or
- be cautioned or charged.

These are, of course, necessary precautions for a vulnerable group of detainees. But, as we have already seen, they also mean that some detainees needing the services of an appropriate adult can be held for disproportionately long periods at the station, especially when a comparison is made with a co-accused, facing the same charges, who does not require such assistance. This lengthy period of detention has implications for the police in that they have to provide extra checks and offer a level of care suitable for the age and distress of the detainee.

Appropriate adults receive no official training. Detainees must be told by the custody officer exactly what the role of the appropriate adult is, but there is no equivalent requirement that an appropriate adult should have their role explained to them, and there is considerable research evidence that questions their effectiveness as a consequence (Dixon 1990; Evans 1993; Evans and Rawsthorne 1994). Where someone experienced in the work is at the station this may conceivably be of less importance, but for those new to the role it means that they may not always act in the best interests of the detainee, and that they are 'acting as appropriate adults in name only' (Bucke and Brown 1997: 69). As we saw in Chapter 4, officers have had to resort to bringing in people from the street to act as appropriate adults, when a detainee has been waiting for attention for a very long time, and it is unlikely that they will be familiar with the task.

At Kilburn there are very few people on hand to act as appropriate adults (should family and social workers be unavailable). Those that we interviewed, three in all, ranged in age from 69 to 80. Two were male and one female. They, like most respondents, were interviewed at the police station. Much is asked of them, in that they frequently have lengthy waits at the station while all the procedures – from booking in, to interview, to charge – are being undertaken. As we shall see, they view this with varying degrees of equanimity and, at times, feel their work is much undervalued. They are volunteers and receive minimal expenses for each visit to the station. Without them the custody staff could not do their work whereas, with the next group we shall be discussing – lay visitors – the work would continue, but would not be subject to outside scrutiny.

Lay visitors

As Home Office research makes clear, the concept of lay visiting was first raised in a Home Affairs Committee recommendation that 'Chief Officers of Police should arrange for sufficient random checks to be carried out to ensure that the procedures are properly observed' (Weatheritt and Vieira 1998: 1). Lord Scarman (in his 1981 report into disturbances in Brixton), added that the safeguards this proposal was intended to introduce 'would be greatly strengthened if it were backed by a statutory system of inspection and supervision of interrogation procedures and detention in police stations' (Scarman 1981, cited in Weatheritt and Vieira 1998: 3–4). When the Home Office finally issued its 1986 circular recommending lay visiting it departed from Lord Scarman's original vision, in that it did not permit lay visitors to be present during interrogations, but it is from these original recommendations that the present system of lay visiting has grown.

The Lay Visitors' Panel in Brent is composed solely of volunteers and, in contrast with some panels, does not include members of the local Police Authority. During the period of this research there were approximately 24 members – reduced to 15 by the end – representative of the many diverse cultures within Brent itself. New members receive a basic training at Kilburn police station and also attend the National Association of Lay Visitors (NALV) training days, which are held at the Metropolitan Police Training School. Lay visitors' appointments are restricted to two three-year terms of office. The scheme is run by an administrator, who is paid for six hours' work per week, and the Panel has ten scheduled meetings per year. Lay visitors are entitled to travel expenses for their work but claiming for them is often problematic, because many rely on public transport and proof of travel is not always readily available. This means that some give up attempts to claim and the Metropolitan Police's reliance on the goodwill of individual lay visitors potentially diminishes the number prepared to undertake the work.

Lay visitors in Brent are responsible for visits to both Kilburn and Wembley police stations and, during the time of this research, aimed to visit Kilburn approximately once a week. (During 2000 42 visits were made.) Their visiting schedules were drawn up some time in advance, which is partially explained by the fact that most members work and it is customary to visit the station in pairs. However, custody staff knew that the Panel's visits were more frequently on either a Sunday or a Monday, so most elements of surprise were lacking. Additionally, over half the visits took place between the hours of 6 and 9 in the evening.[1] The times when cells might be most occupied, such as late at night, were less likely to be times when lay visitors would arrive at the station.

At an earlier stage, several of the Panel's members were also appropriate adults, until the Home Office said their accreditation as lay visitors would be withdrawn if they did not resign from the local services' appropriate adult scheme. (This decision has now been reversed, but there are regulations governing when they may act as either.) This means that some of the appropriate adults whom we interviewed had also had experience of working as a lay visitor, but had been obliged to make a choice between the two roles.

In March 1999 a member of the research team attended one of the Panel's meetings and explained what our research entailed. The panel were initially resistant and indeed somewhat hostile to the research, for reasons which we could not determine. The request for co-operation was later set out formally, asking that we should be allowed to interview members of the Panel. By July 1999 one member had been interviewed.

In April 2000 there was an incident in the Kilburn area and some members of the Panel were asked to attend the station on an emergency basis. This led to the holding of an extraordinary meeting of the Panel and a member of the research team attended on an unofficial basis. She was asked to explain her work and left contact details so that members could alert her to when they might be available for interview. She later received a request that she should again speak to the Panel about the research, but this request was declined because it was felt that sufficient information had already been provided. By the end of the research period a total of five members had been interviewed. Of these, all but one were male and similarly all but one were white (self-defined). Their ages ranged from 35 to 69. With one exception, they had all been lay visitors for four years or longer. All interviews were conducted at the station.

The aftermath of the incident which had led to the holding of the extraordinary meeting had been recorded by the CCTV at Kilburn and the Panel was anxious to know why they had not been allowed to view the relevant tapes. As was clarified at the time, the Protocols in place at Kilburn do not ordinarily permit the viewing of tapes – or monitors – by lay visitors. However, the draft Home Office *Revised Guidance on Lay/ Custody Visiting* (November 2000) would appear to have superseded that, saying:

> where specific incidents or circumstances arise as issues and have been captured on CCTV, visitors might reasonably be allowed access where both the police and detainee(s) concerned consent.

With the consent of a divisional commander or equivalent, lay visitors may now view tapes under the following circumstances:

- a death or other critical incident has occurred involving a person(s) in police custody on [*sic*] their borough;

- as a result of the death or incident serious public disorder is likely;

- showing the video is likely to prevent this public disorder from occurring;

- the interests of public safety in preventing disorder outweigh the possible privacy issues caused by showing the video.

(Metropolitan Police 2001: 16)

Generally, though, lay visitors do not view tapes because of issues of privacy; detainees must give their permission to be observed, as is discussed later in this chapter. This leaves any Lay Visiting Panel, as representatives of the local community, with considerable extra responsibilities.

Forensic medical examiners

As we discussed in Chapter 4, custody officers are faced with immediate decisions when detainees arrive at the station, one of which is whether an FME should be called to examine the new arrival. Under PACE *Codes of Practice*, section C9.2, 'the custody officer must immediately call the police surgeon...if...(a) [the person] appears to be suffering from physical illness or a mental disorder; or (b) is injured; or (c) [Not Used]; or (d) fails to respond normally to questions or conversation (other than through drunkenness alone); or (e) otherwise appears to need medical attention'. Additionally, section C9B of the *Codes* cautions them to 'call the police surgeon when in any doubt, and act with all due speed'. Within the booking area at Kilburn there are notices prominently displayed, alerting officers to medical symptoms which could be misinterpreted, and again urging them to call an FME should they be in any doubt. As a number of our interviewees indicated in Chapter 4, this is an issue which officers take seriously and they prefer to call out an FME – and find it was unnecessary – rather than risk making the wrong decision. Having arrived at the station the FME then has to decide whether the detainee is fit to be detained and/or interviewed.

The role of an FME is not, perhaps, as straightforward as might be imagined. Even the name itself, although used by the Metropolitan Police Service, is not universally used, with some forces preferring to retain the title 'police surgeon'. As Savage *et al.* (1997) explain, 'the role of the police surgeon encompasses a range of often complicated and potentially conflicting tasks' (p. 82). Amongst the various points they make, two have particular relevance to our research: that FMEs act as 'both provider of medical care and gatherer of evidence, clinical or otherwise'; and, that they are 'confronted with competing loyalties between a "doctor–patient" relationship on the one hand and a "doctor–police" relationship on the other' (p. 84). Savage *et al.* (1997) suggest that FMEs might be subject to a conflict of interest should they hear or see information, during the course of their examination, which might be of use to the police, even though the British Medical Association has expressly said that FMEs must treat detained persons as patients and respect confidentiality. The fact that FMEs are employed by the police conceivably throws some doubt on just where their loyalties lie. Whether this is fully understood by the detainee being examined is uncertain and it is likely that some might believe that any consultation remains essentially the same as one conducted outside a police station.

The importance of this relates to the record provided by the cameras. While the FMEs at Kilburn have their own consulting room, which is not covered by the cameras, they also speak to detainees in the cells. Visits are carried out in the company of an officer, so any element of confidentiality is immediately lost. The cell door is generally not shut and conversations may be picked up by the audio-linked corridor cameras, as well as visually by the cell cameras. In light of this the precise role of FMEs becomes even more important should tapes of their supposedly confidential consultations subsequently be used in court proceedings.

In the event, we were only able to interview two FMEs at Kilburn. FMEs appear at the station at frequent intervals but, such is the nature of their work, never to a predictable timetable. There are few of them and they often have to rush to other appointments. Yet their job is of particular importance because it is their judgement which determines whether or not a suspect may be detained or interviewed. The problem inherent in the ill-defined position FMEs occupy has been described by Savage *et al.* (1997) as "clientship"; is the doctor's client the suspect/ detainee as "patient", or the police who request medical assistance?' The presence of the cameras in the custody suite at Kilburn might well require that this question be properly addressed by other police forces contemplating the use of similar technology. FMEs have a particularly important part to play in the running of an efficient custody suite and are relied upon by both detainees and officers as external providers of help and protection.

Visiting the station; co-operation?

The four groups on whom we are focusing attention in this chapter arrive at police stations with different responsibilities. They all have statutory duties, but only the solicitors and FMEs are paid for their work.[2] The arrival of these outsiders in the custody suite evokes varying responses from officers, particularly when given the opportunity to speak specifically about solicitors.

> Certain solicitors can get very picky and patronising and con-descending. I hate that.
>
> (CO 4)

Solicitors' previous experiences of visiting the station can leave them with certain expectations of how they will next be received. The relationships between them and the police can sometimes be fraught, thanks to an underlying suspicion of each party's position.

They understand our role but they resent it. If they think your client is difficult then they can be distinctly grudging in their duties towards you. So much depends on the client and one's own previous history with that sergeant.

(pre S 1)

It varies. The majority are respectful – it's a them and us thing. They think we're obstructing their work. They see themselves as law enforcers – their role is more that of protecting society, but they see themselves as judge and jury. You have to be professional. The more senior they are the better they are.

(S 5)

This suspicion of solicitors is not confined to officers, largely because solicitors are sometimes thought to pay scant regard to the fact that others are giving freely of their time, as this appropriate adult indicates.

I walk in and tell them I don't want to be here all day. I don't get paid, apart from a £10 call out fee – and they [police] get on with it. I hate solicitors. They don't care about keeping you waiting.

(AA 3)

It is not necessarily suspicion that can colour the relationship between officers and these outsiders. A lay visitor might face an officer who knows nothing about them or their role – and it is worth noting that whenever officers were asked to comment on how outsiders might respond to the cameras in the custody suite, they very rarely mentioned lay visitors.

Occasionally we don't get through reception that quickly. I met a chap [officer] about six months ago – just out from Hendon – and he didn't know what lay visitors are. I don't know if they get any training about us.

(LV 2)

But it was not only the officers who failed to comment on the lay visitors. Detainees generally did not recognise the term, so could not speak about them, either. This is recognised by the lay visitors themselves ('98 per cent don't know who we are to start with!' (LV 1)), who need the officers to take them around the cells and introduce them to detainees. (Lay visitors may not approach detainees directly because a detainee who does not wish to speak to them would have had their right to privacy breached.) Consequently, lay visitors are entirely dependent upon the type of introduction effected by the officer – and some of these are inadequate. It is not uncommon for some detainees to refuse to speak to lay visitors and Panel members squarely attribute this to the officer's introduction. Consequently, the Panel are pressing for a standard introduction to be read out. When asked if detainees welcomed their visits, one lay visitor replied:

> Mostly. Some don't want it. In their heart of hearts they may think that seeing us they are doing something against the police. Seventy-five per cent welcome lay visitors. If they are not regular 'visitors' [to the cells] they don't know [about us]. They should be told who we are and to expect us at any time.
>
> (LV 2)

This lack of knowledge confirms one of our other findings; that detainees often do not read (or cannot read) notices posted on the walls, which is why many did not know about the cameras at the station. Directly under the notice saying 'ATTENTION, Notice to all persons in Police detention at Kilburn Police Station' (Figure 5.1), on the wall adjacent to the booking desk, there is another notice, shown in Figure 6.1.

Figure 6.1 Notice about lay visitors displayed in the booking area at Kilburn

---

LAY VISITORS
are independent local people
appointed by the Home Office
to visit Police Station custody areas to ensure
- you are being properly treated;
- your rights have been explained;
- you've had a chance to exercise those rights;
- sanitary facilities are available, cells and bedding are in proper condition, etc.

IF VISITORS CALL WHILE YOU'RE HERE, it is for YOU to decide if you want to speak to them – but please don't hesitate to ask about anything regarding your detention on which you are not sure or satisfied.

ALL INFORMATION ABOUT PEOPLE IN CUSTODY IS KEPT IN STRICT CONFIDENCE BY THESE VISITORS.

It was clear from detainees' replies that they generally knew nothing about lay visitors and had not received a visit from them.

Under PACE, as well as informing detainees of their right to see a solicitor, custody officers also have to decide whether an appropriate adult should be called to the station. If one is required they must be summoned as expeditiously as possible. As we already know, the number of appropriate adults is limited. Should a detainee arrive in the middle of the night and require one, custody staff might decide to delay calling the adult out until the detainee (most frequently a juvenile) has had the sleep to which they are legally entitled. But this is not the only complication related to calling out an appropriate adult, as the following quote makes clear.

> They won't ring in the middle of the night. They wait until about 8 a.m. In the past we would wait for hours for the solicitor. I now ring the custody officer before coming to see when the estimated time of arrival for the solicitor is...With multiple cases we might have to wait until all the interviews are over and all those being charged and it can take ages.
>
> (AA 1)

With solicitors, on the other hand, there is not – and cannot be – this tacit agreement with officers about when they should be called; if a detainee requests a solicitor, one must immediately be called, except in closely prescribed circumstances. Solicitors are sometimes sceptical about how quickly this is done.

> I always check the records when I arrive so I can tell when a client has requested a solicitor – and when I was called. How accurate the record is I will never know – how busy the suite is at the time I will never know...If they are drunk or drugged there can be a delay, but if it's a businessman on a drunk-drive they get on to it right away. It's fairly common to have a 20–30 minute delay.
>
> (S 3)

Officers sometimes see this differently.

> Solicitors should be more accountable. You may read [in the records] that we have requested a Duty Solicitor. Some get a better case in so phone you back and say 'not coming'. They don't think that the suspect has already waited five hours. They may come in and have a two-hour consultation (pay is a consideration) and this

delays the release of a suspect. My responsibility is to treat them [detainees] fairly and efficiently and to get them out *quickly*.

(pre CO 9)

PACE also gives officers clear guidance on the need to contact FMEs and, as we have already seen in Chapter 4, officers tend to call them if in the slightest doubt.

If I feel the FME is required I will call them. I can speak to them on the phone first and get advice. With asthmatics that is possible. If it was a juvenile I would always call the FME.

(CO 7)

Yet there is some resentment of the FMEs, even if their importance is never underestimated, largely because they are thought to be benefiting from the existing call-out system and that, as a consequence, 'they have too many calls to deal with' (CO 7).

Getting the FME has got worse. A lot have dumped their private practice because they can make so much money here – £40 a consultation.

(CO 3)

By contrast, the few FMEs to whom we were able to speak did not complain about the police and found them supportive.

The combined attention of all these groups is focused on the detainees, who at times will complain about their treatment or conditions at the station. Insofar as the solicitors were concerned, some of the complaints (such as not being allowed to smoke) were 'grounded, but might not be possible to avoid' (pre S 3), whereas others were harder either to prove or disprove. As one said, 'complaints have moved to the street, or the back of the van' (S 2). Another solicitor suggested that complaints were more 'to do with the reason for their arrest, rather than their treatment at the station' (S 3). A lay visitor, inevitably, was more concerned with complaints relating to being at the station itself, because that is the extent of their remit, yet understood the difficulties facing the police.

Lack of washing facilities is the most genuine complaint. They need someone standing with them – it's manpower again. It depends on the complaint. Smoking it's 100 per cent true! They complain they aren't allowed a phone call and don't realise a home search means their wife or girlfriend can't be informed. Nothing to read – but some put it down the toilet so the police are in a difficult position. Modern handcuffs hurt. No drugs and none available from the FME at the station.

(LV 1)

Cameras in the booking area

Each of these separate groups, though independent of the police, are reliant upon the assistance and co-operation of the custody officer to get their work done. Custody officers, in turn, find their work increased by virtue of the fact that these outsiders must be at the station. It is against this background of mutual interdependence that we now look at how each group individually reacted to the cameras in the booking area.

Insofar as the cameras affected them personally, lay visitors were largely unbothered: 'you are thinking about the visit and what you are writing down' (LV 1). They knew the cameras were there, but had quickly grown accustomed to them. The appropriate adults reacted in much the same way, while also welcoming the cameras' evidential possibilities 'in case there is trouble' (AA 2). When asked if they thought the cameras might affect the behaviour of the police there was some divergence of opinion, with lay visitors assuming that familiarity with the cameras would soon cause the police to ignore them. Appropriate adults, by contrast, had noticed changes.

Because they [police] know they are being monitored they are a lot more courteous. They are always courteous with us, but juveniles are sometimes very rude and now they [police] are more careful about what they say.

(AA 1)

There are two general reasons for investing some trust in such an account. Firstly, it is largely in line with what was reported by detainees themselves and, secondly, appropriate adults tend to see the police operating for much longer periods than do lay visitors, frequently having enforced time in which to sit and observe procedures while they are waiting for solicitors to arrive, or interviews to take place. Furthermore, this belief in the modified behaviour of the police was largely corroborated by solicitors, though occasionally there was some scepticism about how long it would last.

They are probably more careful about their actions when solicitors or appropriate adults are present. Allegations can now be disproved, thanks to CCTV.

(S 2)

They'd probably have to treat the detainees with a lot more respect and if they do have to use force they would be more careful. Eventually they will completely forget and they will revert. You become immune.

(S 4)

As for the cameras having an influence on their own behaviour, solicitors saw things from a very different perspective. Although they tended to forget about the surveillance when waiting for clients, the cameras had a decisive impact on how they went about their work.

I'm not really aware, except when clients start talking to you in front of the cameras or you have to discuss bail with the custody sergeant. It makes you aware of behaving sensibly and the embarrassment of saying something stupid.

(pre S 3)

I always forget, but am reminded by the screen. It does matter if you are consulting with the client. You have to be aware, to remind the client and yourself not to talk when in camera shot.

(pre S 2)

One solicitor thought the cameras would affect the way in which FMEs conducted consultations.

It may make the lay visitors do a more thorough job. With the FMEs the examination is often not fully done and they make assumptions about patients – CCTV might make them more rigorous. It could be useful to have a tape to prove the state of a client who shouldn't be interviewed, but the FME says is fine. This forces the advice to clients of 'no comment', which has ramifications.

(pre S 4)

Detainees, when asked to think about whether the cameras might affect how these groups behave, tended to concentrate on the solicitors and FMEs. They, generally, could not imagine that they would be anything other than professional in their dealings at the station.

They are professionals and would act in a professional manner.

(p/d 43)

One detainee raised the interesting possibility that the cameras might be used to check the behaviour of the solicitors themselves, reflecting a suggestion made by a jaundiced officer, that 'solicitors should be monitored, they breach their own codes' (CO 1).

> Solicitors are monitored to see how they communicate. In case of illegal dealings, unlawful behaviour.

(p/d 9)

Some detainees also recognised the evidential use of the cameras for FMEs, although the following comment shows a misunderstanding of just how and when the tapes might be viewed.

> If the doctor sees you with any marks he might want to have a quick flick through the film to see how it happened.

(p/d 18)

When these outside groups were asked to imagine how the cameras might modify the behaviour of detainees, they responded almost unanimously by saying that they would make no difference at all. A small number, however, thought the detainees' behaviour might be a little more restrained as a consequence. A solicitor again raised the point about notices alerting them to the cameras, saying 'there are signs everywhere but I doubt it's made any difference to their behaviour. Even the ones that can read don't notice the cameras' (S 4).

The tapes as evidence

At this stage of the interview these respondents were largely echoing the attitudes of both detainees and officers to the cameras in the booking area. No one felt particularly physically unsafe in that area, so the cameras were not thought to be useful to them in that respect. When they came to review the other possible uses of the cameras, most settled on the evidence which they could provide as being most important. One of the solicitors acknowledged that they had been slow in realising the potential of the tapes.

> Nobody seems to request copies of tapes afterwards. It's probably a lack on our part.
>
> (pre S 1)

He was thinking of the way in which the tapes could assist his clients. This was corroborated by an officer who implied that the outcome would generally favour the police, saying 'they [solicitors] haven't got to grip with the tapes. They challenge in court without having asked to see the tapes beforehand' (CO 3).

The solicitors welcomed the fact that the tapes could corroborate versions of events, while accepting that this might not always be the case. They did not, however, think that the cameras afforded any physical protection or that they were in need of it.

> It's a good idea. It's a protection for the defendant. For the police, as well. The downside for the client is that if they kick off there is cast-iron evidence against them.
>
> (S 3)

> I have always felt safe physically. The CCTV can be used against you. The argument can have begun elsewhere and end up in the custody suite so it ends up sounding completely different at the end, out of context. In the past they didn't always enter my representations in the record – and this proves what I said.
>
> (S 2)

A lay visitor also understood the possible powers of the tapes, when referring to a previous event.

> When we were serving our first six years there was a big case and we were summoned to court and all. In a case like that it won't have anything to do with us if we are doing our things right. The cameras would have provided evidence. [There had been an allegation of assault and the police eventually settled out of court.]
>
> (LV 2)

At this point in the interviews there were no concerns raised about privacy and, as just indicated, it was the evidential possibilities of the cameras which were most appreciated. This was succinctly captured by a lay visitor.

A couple of years ago they had a chap who died in Harlesden and I could see it was heading up to be a riot or something. Even now I am not satisfied with the explanation we got. If there had been a camera we would have known.
(LV 2)

Cameras in the cells

Trusting the police

Almost all of those interviewed knew that cameras had been installed in the cells and had some idea of how they might be monitored. Most had had the new system explained to them and, despite the Protocols, one lay visitor had actually been allowed to view the monitor.

> I was there a couple of weeks ago and someone was doing something in the cell and the custody officer said 'see what he is doing'.
>
> (LV 2)

They were aware of the cameras as they went about their work, but there was a noticeable divergence of opinion as to how much of an effect they had. While lay visitors, appropriate adults and solicitors appeared to accept the word of the police that there was no audio link to the cells, solicitors were extremely sceptical.

> I don't like having CCTV on during a consultation. We have been told it's not linked to audio, but other officers have said it is.
>
> (S 2)

> I wouldn't have a consultation in a cell that had a camera. There are concerns within the legal profession about whether that *is* the truth – that there is no audio link. The fact that they have a camera would make me very unhappy about taking instructions there.
>
> (S 3)

As illustrated, some of their scepticism was linked to the mixed messages they were receiving from officers. They simply did not believe that they could not be heard in the cells, which left them – as they saw it – with no alternative but to wait for the one consultation room to be free. Cells, at the best of times, are unpleasant places in which to linger and it is easy to understand why, on a physical level, solicitors would prefer to work in a proper consultation room. Consulting in a cell means that they have to balance paperwork on their knees, while sitting at an awkward angle on the bench if they are to face the detainee. Even the suspicion that they might be observed adds to solicitors' reluctance to enter the cells to talk to clients.

> It happened last week when I said I was not prepared to go into a cell. I said they should provide consultation rooms, otherwise I'd use an interview room. I have never been a fan of going into the cells – it's not conducive to a good consultation.
>
> (S 2)

> Sometimes the interview room isn't available and they say 'use the cells'. You cannot give proper advice. I would not go into the cells now. I don't believe it's not linked to audio.
>
> (S 5)

The solicitors' difficulties were sometimes acknowledged by custody staff.

> With most of the solicitors I would prefer they went to the consultation room. We have to be straight up about no audio link – it only needs to happen once and the Metropolitan Police could not afford the possible bills.
>
> (CO 7)

And detainees.

> You say there is no sound – I've yet to meet my solicitor but I'm sure he would treat it as a complete surveillance unit.
>
> (p/d 21)

The other visitors to the custody suite did not foresee that their work would be affected by the new cameras, although lay visitors raised the point about being personally identifiable, should they be visible on a tape played in court. Some officers suspected that the FMEs might take more trouble with their consultations, just because there was a potential record available.

> The only thing I notice here [with the FMEs] – sometimes they check *more* for responses. They interview more, but it could be just different FMEs.
>
> (CO 11)

Privacy

In common with the officers and detainees, these outside groups were concerned about the lack of privacy for detainees and their worries also centred on the filming of the toilet.

> I have heard from colleagues of cases where people wouldn't go to the toilet. It must have quite a psychological impact.
>
> (LV 3)

Some suggested ways in which the toilet area could be removed from the ambit of the cameras.

> I would like the toilet curtained off.
>
> (AA 1)

> Could I suggest that the toilet is blurred? As we see on TV? It is a serious concern. Strip searches can be a problem.
>
> (AA 2)

As will become clear during the remainder of this chapter, the solicitors we interviewed were largely opposed to the use of cameras within the cells. Those solicitors spoken to following the system's installation replied to questions in the knowledge that the cameras were *in situ*. They sometimes addressed problems that might arise, without endorsing the actual concept of total surveillance. Here, two comment on cross-gender monitoring of the cameras.

> The toilet may cause embarrassment – I wouldn't like it – for women, since most custody officers are men. I might ask for a search to be conducted elsewhere.
>
> (S 6)

> I have a problem with men being able to see women on the toilet and vice versa. It's a question of human rights.
>
> (S 5)

Other solicitors resisted this approach, maintaining their opposition and suggesting that the statutory checks should obviate the need for such surveillance.

They [detainees] would feel very uncomfortable. If it were me I would feel it's a huge invasion of my privacy. I can see safety issues, particularly for vulnerable clients, but they are meant to be checked regularly, anyway.

(S 3)

I think it's wrong, unnecessary, an invasion of privacy. If the police were checking properly then safety wouldn't be an issue.

(S 6)

Protection and evidence

As can be seen from the last quote, interviewees found it difficult to separate the issue of privacy from that of protection and they quite often made the extra connection between the 'camera as source of evidence' and the 'camera as guarantor of protection'.

Their unauthorised visits are now recorded. Allegations by suspects of physical abuse can now be substantiated – or not – so it's less likely to happen.

(S 2)

For searches and the like it's bound to [have an effect]. If cameras can show an officer on the case has gone into a cell for no obvious reasons, they are going to have to justify it – but things have changed a lot in the last 20 years.

(S 3)

The solicitors tended to associate 'protection' with detainees being kept safe from physical harm administered by the police, whereas some of the other interviewees more immediately associated 'protection' with detainees being kept safe from self-harm. In this respect, they all thought the cameras would, to a certain extent, modify the behaviour of the police.

I would think so. Assuming we have a rotten egg, it's going to stop him, I would have thought. Stop them being physical, but I've never heard of a prisoner being beaten up. More importantly, suicides.

(AA 2)

In some cases they may prevent abuse [although] my view is that that is uncommon. It might prevent beatings in cells.

(S 6)

On their own behalf they did not seem to feel unsafe in any part of the station. They appeared confident that officers would warn them if a detainee should not be approached, or that their own commonsense would keep them safe.

I've attended training and I know the boundaries. The custody officer would not allow you in if he thought there was danger.

(LV 3)

I go in there. I don't care. I tell the kids 'behave yourself' and that's it. These kids know more about this business than anyone.

(AA 1)

Clients never want to duff up their defence solicitor – it's the police they want to kill!

(S 4)

As with other respondents, solicitors, appropriate adults and FMEs were asked about what sort of surveillance system ('open' or 'closed') they felt would be most appropriate. No one was happy with the idea of a 'closed' system being installed. One lay visitor thought it possible that 'it might be better for the custody officer because he wouldn't be liable, because he wouldn't be watching'(LV 1), yet still finished with the thought that an open system would be better if there were enough people to do the monitoring. It was precisely the fact that the tapes would not be monitored which alarmed the others, but a solicitor voiced some scepticism as to whether the police might be trusted.

Firstly, you have to take the police at their word – that they aren't viewing it elsewhere. All the same issues apply – invasion of privacy. How do you know what they do with this? A lot of concerns are still there.

(S 3)

That defeats the object, which is to keep an eye more or less at all times. So it's proactive rather than reactive.

(AA 1)

They also dismissed the idea of having just a few cells monitored.

There's no point having that. If it's only in a few it makes the custody officer's job difficult. You can't tell who are the suicidal and the self-harmers. It's difficult.

(LV 1)

It's no good having one in one cell and not in the others. You might as well do the whole lot.

(AA 3)

These respondents saw the cameras as being primarily of use to the police and detainees, rather than themselves (except for evidential purposes). It was one of the FMEs who saw the cameras as being helpful to their own work, in that the monitors would enable officers to supplement the statutory cell checks.

> The observation and constant monitoring would contribute to the health and well-being of the prisoner and may even be life-saving. We'd feel more comfortable telling the police to keep a close eye on a prisoner. At present we feel uncomfortable as they can only do 15–20 minute checks, which is not a close enough monitoring.
>
> (pre FME 1)

However, this FME did not wish to imply that cameras were a solution to the problems surrounding the monitoring of detainees; rather, that they might be an additional resource in face of the reality that some detainees would continue to be held (inappropriately, as he saw it) in the cells.

> CCTV is a very unsatisfactory way to observe people with head injuries or who are drunk, who should really be in hospital. CCTV may help in some ways, but really they shouldn't be in cells in the first place, but in hospital.
>
> (pre FME 1)

When they were asked to think about the effect the cameras might have on the detainees the solicitors were more worried than others about the lack of privacy. Lay visitors and appropriate adults, by contrast, tended to hold a more sanguine view of the nature of privacy and the impact of the cameras.

> We used to have an awful lot of banging and complaining. We don't have that now.
>
> (AA 1)

> There's a spy-hole in the wall, a wicket in the door. Prisoners have been viewed by the police for the last 100 years – it's no different.
>
> (LV 1)

While the wicket and spy-hole appeared to be accepted as confirmation of the general absence of privacy in the cell, with their use being a reminder to detainees that they could be observed at any time, a solicitor employed the same example – of the wicket – to suggest that its use was preferable, because detainees knew when they were being observed, instead of simply fearing they might be.

> Clients have complained. They don't like being constantly monitored. When the wicket goes down you know someone is watching you. Some have asked 'can they see me go to the toilet?' and I don't know if they have blocked that out. Some groups would react differently.
>
> (S 2)

An infringement?

As the following quotes in a sense summarise, the cell cameras appeared to some of these outsiders to have a dual function: they were there to protect as well as provide a record of detention for both detainees and the police.

> It will help both sides – will identify who put plastic cups down the toilet. If there's an argument it will help clarify who is at fault.
>
> (LV 1)

> [They are] for the protection of the custody officers and the detainees and the public at large. You have a record. I don't think there will be any more hangings.
>
> (AA 1)

While solicitors accepted that the cameras indeed did provide a record (and some protection), this did not mean that they accepted the principle of such surveillance. As one remarked 'it offers protection to clients, but it's also degrading' (S 2). Some anticipated that the introduction of the Human Rights Act 1998 would lead to legal challenges.

> The cameras are a complete invasion of privacy and you will have firms of lawyers queuing up to sue the Metropolitan Police over this. The Human Rights Act will make this happen.
>
> (S 4)

This same solicitor again raised the possibility of litigation should the Metropolitan Police decide to extend the scheme to other stations, whereas other solicitors would not even contemplate the possibility of such an extension; they simply disapproved.

> They will be taking a major risk extending it. They will wait until the Human Rights Act comes into effect and see the expense of being sued. Even if they prevent one suicide, can they still justify the expense?
>
> (S 4)

> I would be against extending it. There are other ways to monitor people. The police see it as a means of protecting *themselves*. Most of the police couldn't care less what happened to suspects – they don't have any respect for them. Any incidents that do happen would just be pushed out of the station – into the vans, onto the streets. It won't stop people being beaten up by the police, according to clients.
>
> (S 2)

The lay visitors and appropriate adults, by contrast, supported the idea that the scheme should be extended to other stations.

> It should be used by every station. If it is known to the general public that there is CCTV you will find fewer complaints about police behaviour.
>
> (LV 4)

> I have always asked for more cameras, particularly in more sensitive areas such as Lambeth. Not just for ethnic minorities – for everyone.
>
> (AA 1)

Conclusion

If we now look at four separate quotes we will see something of the way these groups view each other. First, an appropriate adult talking about his relationship with the police.

> I have been so lucky, they are very kind to me. One or two delay me, but I would always say 'you realise we are assisting you'. We are always told that if we are delayed for a long time then you should just walk out. You work under the law of reasonableness.
>
> (AA 2)

Another appropriate adult refers to solicitors.

Get rid of bloody solicitors! We never used to have them, but they suddenly realised they could make loads of money here. I tell them I'm a volunteer.

(AA 3)

A lay visitor considers the detainees.

When I enter the cell I forget about the camera and all I see is the detainee.

(LV 3)

An officer talks about the FMEs and the appropriate adults.

[We would be helped] by having a specifically trained medical expert at the station. The failure of community care means we get them all. If we had someone here who could do some of the things the FME does. The appropriate adult system is shambolic. Why can't we have...as a paid appropriate adult whom we contact at any time without going through Social Services? He should be a Brent employee, but paid by us.

(CO 8)

These outside groups all have to work together, but clearly have reservations about how effective their relationships are. As one lay visitor said of the officers 'we need a partnership where we can trust each other' (LV 3). These relationships are all recorded – and mediated – by the cameras, so they are not divorced from their influence, even when they personally appear untroubled by them. Only the solicitors felt very strongly that the cameras were an unwarranted intrusion into the privacy of their clients. Both the appropriate adults and the lay visitors valued what they assumed was the extra protection afforded detainees by the installation of the cameras, with one raising a further point about access to the tapes, saying 'it's not just the police who should have access to [them]' (LV 3). As we have seen, the whole question of protection was intimately linked to the evidential possibilities of the cameras, yet they did not make the connection, as had both detainees and officers, that this was also linked to public confidence.

The FMEs are faced with an additional problem to the others in that their role is not as clearly defined. Separately, they articulated the same concern.

I would only do a limited examination in a cell....confidentiality could be a problem in a cell.

(FME 1)

> Often we see people in cells – sometimes very aggressive people in the company of an officer...Confidentiality is already compromised by the need to consult prisoners in the presence of an officer, so this [CCTV] would simply add another element of security.
>
> (pre FME 1)

This need for confidentiality is something they share with solicitors, but solicitors are solely answerable to their clients. The unanswered question for solicitors is whether they may trust the police when they are told that the cells are not linked to audio equipment. One conjectured how the police might use the tapes, but not particularly seriously.

> Unless the video is better quality than most, they couldn't lip read. It would be easier to bug the cells. They don't have the personnel to watch the monitors all the time.
>
> (S 1)

As we have been writing this, three men have been convicted of murder at Teesside Crown Court as the result of a prison cell having been 'bugged' by the police. This is the first time that a British court has accepted evidence obtained from a bugged cell. Additional evidence against one of the accused was obtained because the police employed a lip reader to decipher videotapes of his conversations. Further, the High Court has agreed to hear claims from two young men that 'their right to a fair trial was breached by the lack of facilities in the stations in which they were held' (Burrell, *The Independent* 10 February 2001). One alleges that he had to speak to his solicitor in 'a filthy cell with no furniture' and the other 'claims he had to telephone his solicitor in the presence of three police officers'.

These three cases relate to some of the central issues we have been discussing; privacy, the cameras as a potential source of evidence, and confidentiality. And, as some of the voices of doctors, solicitors, lay visitors and others in this study have demonstrated, being able to trust the police to administer the system honestly is of paramount importance. In the following chapter we shall draw these strands together and offer some of our own conclusions.

Notes

1 Brent Lay Visiting Panel 13th Annual Report
2 Appropriate adults receive a token payment to cover costs of travel, if the referral has come through the Social Services, and lay visitors also receive minimal travel costs.

Chapter 7

Conclusion: policing, CCTV and social control

Everywhere the State acquires more and more direct control over the humblest members of the community and a more exclusive power of governing each of them in his smallest concerns. This gradual weakening of the individual in relation to society at large may be traced to a thousand things.

(Alexis de Tocqueville 1835)

The installation of CCTV cameras in the cells at Kilburn police station forces us to consider contemporary surveillance in a somewhat unusual setting. It does so for a number of reasons.

Firstly, the bulk of criminological concern to date has focused on the use of CCTV in public space. This is not surprising given the concentration of CCTV in public space in the UK. Indeed, we are somewhat unusual in this regard. There is nowhere that compares with the UK in its use of CCTV. The United States, often considered to be the test-bed for developments in social control, has until recently had comparatively little CCTV in the public spaces of its city and town centres. CCTV is much more likely to be found in the privatised urban spaces of the US: the shopping malls, gated communities and other enclaves and protected spaces (Davis 1998). In both continental Europe and Australasia, the use of CCTV in public space also does not compare with the UK (Lyon 2000; Fox 2001).

Secondly, although the custody suite is not 'public space' in the standard sense, neither is it prototypically 'private'. Access to the custody suite is carefully regulated, though there is often a fairly constant flow of people passing through. One of the key themes in the surveillance literature concerns the impact of CCTV on privacy. Again, however, the nature of the custody suite in general, and the cell in particular, provides a very different set of circumstances from those normally considered in thinking about the consequences for privacy. Related to this, the Kilburn experiment provides an unusual, but arguably informative, arena in which to consider certain much-discussed human rights issues pertaining to prisoners. The protection of privacy and the limits of covert policing have been considered by lawyers and other commentators at some length (Justice 1998). The Kilburn case raises questions in relation to the protection of privacy and the use of *overt* surveillance. Furthermore, it provides a particularly clear case in which to consider how the protection of privacy may be sustained alongside the right to life. These two fundamental tenets of the Human Rights Act are, as this book has made clear, not necessarily always compatible.

Thirdly, much of the literature on surveillance, for understandable reasons, makes a fairly clear distinction between those being 'watched' and those doing the 'watching'. As we have described, this distinction is by no means so clear-cut in the case of the custody suite. Thus, whilst prisoners are watched by police officers, the officers themselves are filmed – and potentially watched – whilst doing the watching. The installation of electronic surveillance in a custody suite turns watchers into the watched. If we view 'surveillance as a form of power', as Norris and Armstrong (1999: 10) suggest we should, how does the complicated nature of surveillance within the custody suite affect power relations?

Fourthly, and related to the third point, the nature of the Kilburn experiment also raises some questions about the governance of the police. At the most basic level it requires us to think about the usefulness of CCTV as a means of affecting the behaviour of police officers. For several decades there has been public and official concern about the treatment of suspects in custody and, more particularly, about how their rights might be protected. Far-reaching legislation, and associated *Codes of Practice*, were introduced in the early 1980s. The *Codes* have been revised several times since and lay visitors have subsequently been introduced. Yet concerns about police behaviour within police stations persist and, moreover, there is little sense that the means for improving civilian, democratic oversight of police treatment of prisoners exist. Might CCTV, as well as having an impact on police compliance with PACE for example, also provide a new means for civic governance of the police?

Fifthly, the nature of the Kilburn experiment illustrates, in a new setting, the Janus-faced nature of electronic surveillance. This can be illustrated in a number of ways. For example, is it the case that CCTV in police cells is primarily to be understood as a further means of controlling and supervising the behaviour and bodies of prisoners? Is it, in these terms, to be understood mainly as a further extension and elaboration of contemporary forms of social control? Or, given what we know about the history of mistreatment of prisoners by the police, particularly those from minority ethnic communities, should CCTV be understood as a means of protecting the vulnerable from harm? Put another way, is our normative frame of reference for understanding such a development primarily a positive or negative one? We raise this, in these terms because, in our view, much contemporary sociological and criminological discourse surrounding CCTV has been, implicitly or otherwise, largely negative in character. Contemporary academic writing has tended to view the proliferation of CCTV as intrusive and damaging to freedoms. At the very least, in our view, it is unhelpful to think of CCTV as if it has only one face.

Sixthly, the CCTV experiment also provides another setting in which to explore the relationship between police and the spread of new technologies. A number of criminologists have talked at length about the impact of new technologies on both the focus and style of contemporary policing (see, for example, Ericson and Haggerty 1997). Many such writers focus on the fairly radical impact that they posit such technologies are having on police work. The use of CCTV within custody suites marries (relatively) new technology with an arena of traditional police work: the 'care' of prisoners. In this book we have considered the impact of such technology on 'policing'. Here we also wish to raise some questions about what this tells us about the contemporary sociology of policing.

Finally, this study raises a host of practical and policy questions about whether and – if so – how CCTV should be used within the custody suite. CCTV cameras are now being installed in the booking areas of many custody suites in police stations in England and Wales. In addition, although they remain relatively few, it is increasingly the case that forces, following the recommendations of the PCA, are installing cameras in a limited number of cells designated for holding particularly vulnerable prisoners. Should CCTV be used at all within custody suites? If so, how extensive should it be? What protection should exist? In a postscript we conclude by considering these and other practical questions, and make a number of recommendations about future use of CCTV in police stations.

CCTV and public and private space

As we outlined in Chapter 1, the rapid proliferation of CCTV in the 1980s, and particularly in the 1990s, is something which distinguishes the UK from the majority of the rest of the developed economies (De Waard 1999). Though CCTV is by no means confined to major public spaces such as town centres, it is now so widespread that it appears that all major cities and most sizeable towns have CCTV surveillance of their public spaces. Perhaps not surprisingly, therefore, the bulk of contemporary writing on CCTV focuses on public space. There is, by contrast, relatively little focus on the use of CCTV in private space, the only exception being work focusing on shopping centres – generally better thought of as 'hybrid space' (see Jones and Newburn 1998). The social circumstances of the custody suite are obviously somewhat removed from what generally pertains in public space.

One perhaps obvious but nonetheless important point that we wish to note, therefore, is that in attempting to understand the uses and consequences of CCTV, it should not be assumed that the study of its application in public space is sufficient. The issues raised by the use and experience of CCTV in the custody suite are in some respects similar to those arising from the use of electronic surveillance elsewhere. However, there are also some potentially instructive points of departure. The first concerns the explicit and symbolic functions of CCTV, the second the possible unintended consequences, and the third the economic rationale.

The first and obvious point to make is that CCTV may perform different functions under different circumstances. Moreover, its functions may also be presented in different ways in order to justify its use. Thus, within the custody suite CCTV was 'sold' on a different basis from that on which public space systems are generally promoted. The rise of town centre CCTV, for example, has generally been underpinned 'by its image as the latest "silver bullet" of crime prevention' (Bannister *et al.* 1998). By contrast, CCTV within the custody suite was publicly 'sold' partly as a means of preventing 'harm' and, internally, partly as a means of providing protection to police officers (against malicious claims, for example).

The explicit purposes of CCTV in these different contexts clearly differ in some respects. CCTV in public space is generally evaluated (and therefore understood) in terms of its efficacy in preventing crime (Tilley 1998) – though obviously it has other purposes. CCTV in the custody suite, by contrast, though sharing some of these 'other' purposes – deterrence, fear reduction, order maintenance – has crime prevention very much as a subsidiary to its primary concerns. It has a crime prevention function but, for a number of reasons, it is not a function that is accorded primacy.

The second point is that one of the suggested effects of the use of CCTV in public spaces has been a consequential decline in the informal social controls that, it is supposed, were previously crucial to the maintenance of public order (Graham *et al.* 1996). Jane Jacobs perhaps most famously described such informal controls:

> The public peace – the sidewalk and street peace – of cities is not kept primarily by the police, necessary as police are. It is kept primarily by an intricate, almost unconscious, network of voluntary controls and standards among the people themselves, and enforced by the people themselves... No amount of police can enforce civilization where the normal, casual enforcement of it has broken down.
>
> (Jacobs 1961: 31–2)

It is not clear that the social order of the custody suite ever worked in quite this way. Arguably, and unlike many other environments, including prison, the nature of power relations in the custody suite is such that order can largely be maintained irrespective of the degree of compliance of prisoners. Thus, the nature of the space (and the population) being watched may have a significant impact on the unintended consequences of the introduction and use of CCTV. More particularly, where one of the unintended outcomes of CCTV in public spaces may be to reduce certain aspects of informal social control, this is unlikely within the custody suite. The reason for this is, primarily, that such 'informal controls' have already been undermined by the introduction of very significant, and highly formalised, procedures in the form of PACE and its associated *Codes of Practice*. If anything, the introduction of CCTV is likely to formalise procedures further. It is possible in fact that the introduction of cameras might eventually allow some officers to avoid elements of formal procedure – such as checking cells in person – and instead rely on cameras, should the *Codes of Practice* be amended to permit this.

Thirdly, the 'economic agenda', to the extent that there is one, underpinning the use of CCTV in the custody suite is markedly different from that in evidence in the use of such surveillance in public space. In town centres, it is argued, the proliferation of CCTV systems has been part of a wider effort to reinvigorate the financial and economic health of such areas. In ·this argument, providing security for businesses and consumers – in part by excluding 'flawed consumers' – is central to the success of town centre CCTV. Clearly, there is no such imperative for the police and custody suite CCTV – with one caveat. That is, in recent years police forces, especially the Metropolitan Police, have been subjected to an increasing number of claims for damages in the courts. In part, this reflects a trend towards increased litigiousness in British society generally. More particularly, it is part of a general decline in the legitimacy of the police and an increased public willingness to challenge both their behaviour and their decision-making. Recognition of these trends was instrumental (albeit in a minor way) in the decision to introduce cameras at Kilburn.

Where there is a very clear similarity in the introduction of CCTV in these different spaces is in connection with the centrality of the 'symbolic' message being conveyed. Thus, local authorities use CCTV in town centres, at least in part, because it promotes the *idea* that such spaces are safer as a result (irrespective of the reality). The point here is that a message can be passed to local communities, or those parts that the local authority particularly wishes to reach, that something is being done – which costs a lot of money, which is modern and which is 'proven' – that will ensure public safety. In the case of Kilburn, the symbolic message for local communities focused on the protection of prisoners; the aim was to bolster trust in the police. As the Borough Commander put it: 'It did serve, for the people I was talking to, as a sign of good faith, goodwill and to help see through something that had been promised to the community...People commented to me on how they didn't think we'd do it.' In both cases the symbolic power of CCTV is at least as important as any 'real' effect it may have.

CCTV and privacy

As the discussion in previous chapters should have made clear, while there is no doubt that increasing surveillance through the use of CCTV implies an increased intrusiveness into the 'private space' of the cell, interviews with suspects in the cells emphasised the highly contingent nature of the 'privacy' available to them – even when cameras were not present.

Reiss (1987: 20) defines 'privacy as places, spaces and matters upon or into which others may not normally intrude without the consent of the person or organization to whom they are designated as belonging'. Whilst the issue of 'belonging' or ownership is a problematic one in the context of a custody suite, it is surely clear that the cell is not a place or space in which the detainee has much privacy. There are three possible views into the cell which do not involve opening the door, and under PACE (1984) gaolers are expected to make regular checks on the well-being of detainees by looking through one of two peep-holes or the wicket. A detainee has no control over when he or she can be seen, and cannot determine who it is that sees them. A detainee has no control over the opening and closing of the cell door, and has no power to invite anyone into the cell or expel anyone from the cell (with the exception of lay visitors and solicitors). They have no independent and autonomous contact with the world beyond the gaoler or custody officers. A detainee has no control over the design and management of the cell environment – there is no furniture to rearrange, no decoration to be done, no personal touch to be varied; indeed the cell is designed specifically to minimise the detainee's autonomous control over the room or its few contents. In the words of one detainee:

> There's no privacy in a cell anyway. In a police station, your privacy is taken away. It would be different in the street.
>
> (pre p/d 10)

Sanders argues that PACE cedes most practical power to the police, so that once someone is detained in police custody, 'the rule of law is jeopardized, due process is made unviable and human rights norms are tested to their limits' (1997: 1068). This is also simply the most practical effect of police arrest, and it is the very reason that a detainee's rights have to be so closely safeguarded.

Inherent in the deprivation of liberty is the loss of autonomy and the suspension of most rights that ordinarily are taken for granted. It might be argued that from the moment that arrestees are prevented from moving freely (i.e. handcuffed), through the process of confirming their identity, the search of their belongings in close detail in the presence of whoever happens to be in the custody area, the intrusiveness of a strip search, the possible removal of their clothes, up to their placement in a locked cell, layer after layer of 'privacy' is removed. The cell, under such circumstances is a very unusual form of space. It is clearly not 'private' in Reiss's terms, for there is considerable intrusion. However, there is very clearly restricted access. The cell, with the degree of surveillance required under PACE for the protection of the suspect, is probably best conceived of as 'hybrid space', i.e. space which exists somewhere on a continuum between 'public' and 'private' (see Jones and Newburn 1998 for a discussion of 'hybrid space').

One important point clearly illustrated by the responses of detainees to questions about the impact of in-cell CCTV was the absence of a uniform set of perceptions and expectations of 'privacy'. There were significant areas of agreement; yet considerable variation was also visible.

The major worry, and the most significant form of intrusion, concerned the filming of the toilet area in the cell. The majority of detainees found this to be particularly intrusive, especially female detainees. However – and it is a very significant caveat indeed – the majority of detainees recognised that the possibility of protection came at a price; that of reduced privacy. Moreover, they were generally prepared to forfeit some of their right to privacy (such as it is) in order to bolster the protection available to them.

This, we think, is an important finding. The Human Rights Act provides both for a 'right to life' (Article 2) and a 'right to a private life' (Article 8). It is recognised that these two rights may come into conflict. As we outlined in Chapter 2, the Metropolitan Police were concerned that if they introduced continuously-monitored CCTV into the cells they might be challenged in the courts for infringements in relation to Article 8. Were this to happen, it would be for the court to consider how to balance the requirements of Articles 2 and 8. The results of this research suggest very clearly that detainees are more worried about what might happen to them whilst they are held in custody than they are about the lack of privacy, unpleasant though the latter may be.

It may be necessary, therefore, to accept a reduction in privacy as a necessary means of providing more effective safeguards for the well-being of detainees. Currently, standards are outlined by PACE and its *Codes of Practice* and monitored using custody records. Despite generally high standards of care, however, there is evidence that records kept by the police are not a reassuring safeguard for suspects fearful of police abuse (McConville *et al.* 1991), as was evident in the case of Marlon Downes.

PACE, creating the role of custody officer, sought to introduce a degree of independence or distance between that role and arresting officers or those conducting interrogations. As far as detainees are concerned it would appear that this is not a distinction that is terribly meaningful; many remain deeply distrustful of all police officers. In this study, it was clear that this absence of trust was extended to the 'management' of the CCTV system. For detainees to feel that CCTV in cells was truly a safeguard, they would need to feel confident that there was no possibility of police tampering with the recording by the cameras. What they required, therefore, was a set of safeguards that would effectively monitor the actions of the police. To an extent, CCTV provided this. It was perceived as being at least a partially effective means of governing the behaviour of the police themselves. In this manner the police were seen to be 'watched' as much as the suspects, and it was that parity which gave the system its credibility. Put another way, as far as detainees were concerned, the protection of their well-being could only be achieved by monitoring or watching the behaviour of police officers.

The supervisors and the supervised

One key objective of the installation of CCTV in custody areas is to minimise the risk of suspects suffering injury (brought about by themselves, by another, or by natural causes) in the first place, and then to account clearly for those situations where harm has been sustained. It can, therefore, be seen as a further addition to the panoply of technologies used in 'risk communication' (Ericson and Haggerty 1997). The introduction of CCTV within the cell area and the cells themselves further illustrates Ericson and Haggerty's (1997: 56) contention that 'coincident with the surveillance of suspect citizens is the surveillance of the police as a suspect population... This surveillance arises out of distrust which is endemic in risk society'. However, it is worth noting that the 'asymmetry of power' generally seen as implicit in CCTV surveillance of public space (Norris *et al.* 1998: 5) could, in some respects, be reversed in the context of the custody suite. Within the custody suite it is not only the prisoner who is 'watched' but the police officer.

The transposition of police officers from 'watchers' to 'watched' (at least retrospectively) is an inevitable consequence of using CCTV to monitor custody suites. The system has considerable potential to monitor, and reduce the risk of, police misbehaviour. In this way CCTV intrudes into the 'private space' of the custody suite; invades what has traditionally been a problematically private sphere of police operation. Indeed, being seen to increase surveillance over police officers via new technological means was integral to the development of this pilot project. From the point of view of the Metropolitan Police this was the most likely means of challenging the widely held negative and distrustful views common within the local community. However, attempts to increase trust via extensions of surveillance inevitably have an impact on the extent of privacy:

> Organizations are known by and trusted because of routinized auditing techniques and forms of accountability. Privacy can expand only with trust, but trust can expand only with surveillance. In summary, accompanying surveillance is a greater intrusion into privacy so that people can be known in risk management

terms...The more often surveillance mechanisms must be used to create trust, the greater is the realization that trust is doubtful. The greater the presumption of trust, the greater the space for surveillance and so on, in an amplifying spiral.

(Ericson and Haggerty 1997: 117)

The Metropolitan Police have a legal responsibility to protect the health and well-being of suspects. There are occasions when, far from doing so, they are accused of directly harming the health or well-being of suspects. Indeed, on a general level it is clear that often they are not trusted by the local community to treat suspects in custody with due care and attention. CCTV becomes a potential 'solution'. The logic here is as follows: if the usual monitoring and investigation of police actions is neither independent nor distanced enough to be credible for community groups and detainees, then the remote and technological distanciation (Giddens 1985) of a CCTV system might provide some more credible means of accountability. However, such surveillance can only be a comfort to detainees if it watches the space occupied by custodians and is tamper-proof. The increase in surveillance, therefore, means that the 'privacy' which is intruded upon is not just that of the detainee in a cell, but also that of the custodian in a police station. Custody officers clearly recognise this dynamic.

This highlights one of the key differences between the use of cameras in the Kilburn experiment and their traditional use in town centres and the like – this involves the 'watchers' themselves. For in the case of the custody suite, as we illustrated in detail, the watchers are also the watched (it is not that this cannot and does not happen elsewhere, merely that it is unusual). In this regard, CCTV shares some of the characteristics of other technologies, for as Ericson and Haggerty point out:

...in the very process of using communication technologies to accomplish their work, police officers are subject to the surveillance capacities of those technologies, which are able to monitor and risk-profile officer conduct in greater detail than human supervisors can.

(1997: 394)

Thus, the introduction of CCTV to the cells at Kilburn is intended not only to allow police officers continuously to monitor suspects in their cells, it is also intended to record the behaviour of the police officers themselves (although only the latter was implicit in explanations provided by the police to the local community). Johnston (2000) has argued that under late modern conditions policing shifts from focusing primarily on communities of collective sentiment to *communities of risk*. These are 'not merely [communities] at risk from some external threat...they are increasingly defined, orientated, organised and governed around matters of security and risk' (2000: 55). One of the lessons of the Kilburn experiment is that, in such terms, police officers are every bit as much a 'community of risk' as 'suspects'. This is a reminder of Peter Manning's observation 'that the primary, abiding and most persistent problems facing Anglo-American policing from its inception in 1829 have been proper internal control, discipline and supervision' (1983: 169). Being clearer about its dual function at the time the CCTV system was introduced might arguably have made it more palatable to most concerned (including officers for whom its purposes would, at least, have been transparent).

In this regard the custody suite differs from many other sites of surveillance. Here the supervisors are also supervised. Thus, in one important respect the officer and the prisoner now have a shared experience of life in the custody suite; they can both be watched. In other respects, however, the generally asymmetrical power relationships that characterise surveillance (Norris and Armstrong 1998) remain largely undisturbed. As Norris and Armstrong put it, whilst 'the watcher can see the watched, the reverse is not true' (1998: 5). This also holds for the custody suite. Whilst prisoners are watched by police officers, prisoners cannot watch police officers. Or, more accurately, they cannot do so in real time. However, they may know that police officers are being filmed, and therefore understand that there is the possibility that they – or their representative – might be able to watch video material of police activity retrospectively.

As detainees suggested in interview, they felt this possibility had already begun to change the nature of relationships within the custody suite. Police officers, they suggested, were more careful about what they did and, particularly, about what they said. Indeed, many officers confirmed that one of the consequences of the installation of cameras had been a further boost to the standards of professionalism visible within the custody suite.

CCTV and the governance of the police

One of the key characteristics of 'late modernity' is held to be the separation of time from space. This 'distanciation' is made possible by new forms of communication, the new 'technologies of life' (Lash 2000). Similarly, watching via CCTV is 'distanciated', i.e. those watching are removed, spatially, from those being watched. The panopticon no longer requires spatial proximity (Bauman 2000). Indeed, Bauman argues that such distanciation is perhaps the key characteristic of late modernity and, really, is what makes late modernity 'post-panoptical'. This has important consequences for social relationships. According to Bauman:

> The end of Panopticon augurs the end of *the era of mutual engagement*: between the supervisors and the supervised, capital and labour, leaders and their followers, armies at war. The prime technique of power is now escape, slippage, elision, and avoidance, the effective rejection of any territorial confinement with cumbersome corollaries of order-building, order-maintenance and the responsibility for the consequences of it all as well as of the necessity to bear their costs.
>
> (2000: 11)

Though the technology could make it possible, the nature of the custody suite – at least as currently organised – is not yet post-panoptical. For legal and organisational reasons the watcher and watched remain in close proximity. It is the same officers, required by PACE physically to monitor the welfare of prisoners, who are tasked with watching the CCTV screens. As such the custody suite in Kilburn resembles, in some important respects, an electronic panopticon; it is something which can 'see constantly and recognise immediately' (Foucault 1977: 200). Clearly, however, it need not remain so. The monitors screening the images from the cells and custody suite could be sited elsewhere. Indeed, in theory the cameras could be monitored by someone other than the police (though this has not as yet been explicitly considered). Retrospectively this already occurs; lay visitors, solicitors and others have access (under limited circumstances) to tapes.

More intriguingly, the technology offers the possibility of 'real time' independent scrutiny; the public could watch the police. To our knowledge this has not previously been suggested as a possibility. So unusual would the suggestion be that the 'citizen' could watch the state that it appears almost illegitimate – almost impossible. But why should it be so? Moreover, if, in Kilburn as elsewhere, one of the major concerns relates to perceptions in the local community about the mistreatment of suspects in custody, do the cameras not provide a means of helping directly overcome such distrust?

Within the Metropolitan Police one of the current fashions is to appoint 'independent advisory groups' whose role is to advise – and, also in some ways provide legitimacy for – certain areas of police activity. In this manner it would be possible, in theory, to form an independent advisory committee that would scrutinise, using CCTV footage, activities in the custody suite. This would, in effect, be an electronic extension of the lay visiting scheme. This in itself would have further implications in relation to privacy (suspects might, rightly, be particularly concerned about 'outsiders' viewing the tapes), but is not, in principle, impossible.

In our view, therefore, the installation of cameras in the custody suite opens up a form of police governance that has rarely been considered previously, if at all. In doing so, it demonstrates also the existence of a 'face' of surveillance that has generally remained invisible to criminologists. The major criminological discourse within which the new surveillance technologies have been understood has been predominantly Orwellian in tone. It has, often for good reasons, talked mainly of the increased reach of the state, of rule at a distance, and of 'responsibilisation' (Garland 1996). In the case of the custody suite, however, there is the possibility of using the technology to monitor the actions of state officials. At the very least, this should lead us to be careful about the language we use to describe the uses and consequences of CCTV.

Against dystopianism

There is an inclination toward dystopianism within contemporary criminological literature on surveillance. There is a tendency to talk of the 'maximum security society' (Marx 1988; Norris and Armstrong 1999), 'big brother' (Davies 1998) and to use Cohen's metaphor of a further 'thinning and strengthening of the mesh', and 'widening of the size and reach of the net' of social control (Cohen 1985). To take such a position is to adopt a particular normative stance in relation to the 'new surveillance'. Within this stance, the possibility that such techniques may have positive consequences is (at best) minimised. That such surveillance might be a part of, might have a useful role to play in, what might normatively be considered to be the 'good society' is rendered impossible.

By contrast, David Lyon (1994) quite rightly argues that surveillance shows more than one face. He says the prominent paradox is 'that surveillance simultaneously represents both a means of social control and a means of ensuring that citizens' rights are respected' (Lyon 1994: 219). This is the position that, we would like to argue, clearly holds for the

Kilburn experiment. It is not only a means of social control of prisoners, it is also a system installed with the avowed aim of increasing the protection of the rights of prisoners (albeit through the social control of police officers and other prisoners).

In drawing such a conclusion we do not wish to dismiss the extent to which the system introduced at Kilburn is intrusive; it is clearly enormously so. However, in accepting this it would still be very misleading to think of the system simply as some dystopian form of maximum surveillance. This, the closest we have in the UK to the 'electronic panopticon', has more than one face. It holds out the possibility of gain and improvement as well as containing some obvious dangers. This is an important corrective to much current criminology which, in its understandable scepticism about many of the claims made on behalf of CCTV by politicians and policy-makers, has tended to assume that the possibilities opened up by such technologies are generally malign, rather than benign or even advantageous.

In attempting to capture the dual nature of CCTV, Jock Young recently argued that it:

> is undoubtedly one of the most invidious of inventions. In the wrong hands it can police factories in a minute and draconian fashion ('the boss is everywhere'), it can generate a web of surveillance which far exceeds anything that is historically known, it can invade privacy and make Orwell's *1984* a reality. But it can also, in a different political context, be liberating and protective.
>
> (1999: 192)

Young's description, though it also places much greater emphasis on the negative, is essentially correct. Technologies such as CCTV may, at least in theory, be socially beneficial as well as potentially harmful. However, whilst concurring with Young's general observation about the ability of CCTV both to intrude and to protect, we wish also to argue that it can do both of these simultaneously in the same political context – not merely in different political contexts. Electronic surveillance is multi-dimensional in its functions and capabilities. Thus, as we have already outlined, one of the key issues for the Kilburn experiment concerns the balancing of the rights to privacy and protection.[1] We have come to accept that these two competing claims are sometimes irreconcilable and that under some circumstances one must, inevitably, have primacy over the other. This is recognised in the Human Rights Act. The loss of dignity occasioned by the loss of privacy should never be underestimated or ignored. The very real subjects of the Kilburn experiment spoke about the intrusiveness of

CCTV and their feelings about being observed. However, one of the key initial reasons for the Kilburn experiment was to increase the protection of detainees. The prisoners themselves recognised that the possibility of increased protection could only come at a cost to their privacy (limited as that already was). By and large this was something they were prepared to accept.

The fact that prisoners recognised this dilemma and were prepared to trade privacy for protection, strikes us as compelling evidence in support of the use of CCTV in this context and in this way. Achieving a reasonable balance, or tension, between privacy and protection is far from straightforward. However, the tension, and the multiple functions that underpin it, are central and inevitable characteristics of the use of electronic surveillance in this context. Recognising this provides the basis for a fuller and more rounded understanding of the potential of such technologies.

Note

1 There has been some scepticism about whether the safety of detainees was the sole reason for installing CCTV. The possibility that tapes might be used in court to provide evidence against detainees cannot be discounted but at this stage we cannot say if that has been the case. We also do not know if the tapes have been used to corroborate detainees' complaints against the police. Anecdotally we are aware that tapes have been shown to solicitors to disprove a detainee's allegation, but we cannot say if that has led to a decline in complaints against the police. We hope that such information will be recorded and disseminated by the police.

Chapter 8

Postscript: using CCTV in the custody suite

When the installation of cell cameras was first discussed within the Metropolitan Police a briefing paper suggested that 'the involvement of external academic evaluation is seen as essential to this project in order to gain a wider perspective of the benefits and outcomes from the equipment used and to provide impartial evidence of the impact from within the local community'.[1] The research reported here raised sociological questions and issues about how we use and how we think and talk about the use of CCTV.

In addition, however, the research was also evaluative. One of its aims was to consider the impact of the introduction of in-cell CCTV and to report on its use and its efficacy. The word 'evaluation' was used in each of the interviews we conducted and in numerous informal conversations with members of the custody staff, keen to establish our reasons for being at the station. These officers frequently emphasised their hopes that our research would be considered widely within the Metropolitan Police in particular, as well as other forces. They felt that their voices were insufficiently heard through more conventional channels and that the installation of the cell cameras raised questions about detainee care – and their own responsibilities – which needed to be widely reflected upon. Detainees were equally keen that surveillance equipment should not be installed without full consideration of the many issues involved, particularly those relating to privacy and protection. Indeed, all of the groups we interviewed hoped that their contributions would be noted, yet predictably many were sceptical that their voices would eventually be heard.

As police forces take up the challenge issued by the Police Complaints Authority to install cell cameras, albeit on a limited scale, there is a need for well-informed debate about the consequences of different ways of implementing CCTV using, where possible, research evidence. In this regard, this study – the only one to our knowledge to be based primarily on interviews with officers and prisoners – provides a sounder basis for consideration of the implications of CCTV than some of the smaller-scale, internal police 'evaluations' such as that conducted by the Devon and Cornwall Constabulary.

The experiment at Kilburn police station has, inevitably, raised issues specific to the station itself. We believe, however, that most of these issues have a wider application and that there are practical difficulties associated with the scheme which require practical solutions. We now look more closely at the points which emerged during the course of our research. The conclusions we reach are informed by the voices of those whom we interviewed. They are also based on the assumption that the use of electronic surveillance within the custody suite is something that is likely to expand, but that tape recording might be superseded by other technology.

Conclusions and recommendations

Training

When new surveillance systems are installed it is essential that staff are adequately trained in their use. It is insufficient to rely on members of individual custody teams to explain to other colleagues how the system works, as this is no guarantee that the system will be explained fully or properly. As we discovered, such a policy of on-the-job instruction can leave officers unsure of how they could adjust monitors so as to use them to their best advantage and, even at the end of the research period, confusion about the scope of the system remained. Additionally, some staff were initially unaware of the Protocols governing the use of the cell-based system.

We suggest that:

- all staff working in a custody suite should be instructed, by a qualified trainer, in the use of the chosen CCTV system and that officers should not be working at the custody desk without such training;

- staff should be made aware of any Protocols or agreements governing the running of such systems.

Tape removal

The integrity of any CCTV system is dependent upon the safe removal and replacement of tapes (and the transparency of this system). Without the tapes there is no record of events. We noted that officers sometimes mistakenly reinserted tapes which they had just removed from the recording machine. Although mistakes cannot altogether be avoided, officers should be instructed that as each tape is removed they must label it immediately, insert it in its sleeve and seal it. Only then should a new tape be inserted in the machine.

At Kilburn the tapes were then taken to a cupboard in the property room, to await collection by the property store staff. This cupboard was also used to store other items and was opened frequently each day. Theoretically the tapes could be lost, in the same way that detainees' property sometimes allegedly went missing. Losses of tapes would crucially undermine public confidence in the CCTV system should tapes of disputed incidents go missing. The very fact that this potential so obviously exists is not likely to instil public confidence. A sealed 'ballot-type' storage box would help resolve this. It should be placed next to the machine housing the video recording equipment. Nothing else should be stored in it and nominated staff should be responsible for its clearance. There would be the added evidential protection for officers of being filmed as they placed each tape inside.

We suggest that:

- staff should be fully trained in the correct method of removing tapes from the recording machine. This training would be part of the overall instruction provided in the use of the CCTV system;

- a sealed 'ballot-type' storage box, placed alongside the video recording machine, should be used for the storage of tapes until they are removed to the property store.

Tape storage

The need to keep tapes for evidential purposes suggests that, should the present use of video continue, problems may well arise with both storage and possible tape deterioration. At Kilburn tapes are stored in metal cabinets; the room presently used for storage is not temperature-controlled and becomes extremely hot during the summer. This is an issue on which the Metropolitan Police should seek technical advice.

We suggest that:

- technical advice should be sought on the best means of storing and preserving tapes.

The extent of the videoing

Discussions with officers revealed that, having become accustomed to the scheme, they were generally happy with the extent of the booking-in area CCTV at Kilburn. There were, however, two reservations. Officers wanted more areas where detainees are dealt with to be under the surveillance of the cameras. For example, at Kilburn the evidential breath room was not videoed and, as this was a room often used by intoxicated detainees, officers feared the risk of an unrecorded incident. A taped record of events would answer any public concerns and help officers to feel more secure professionally.

This concern also applied to the property room as, on occasion, detainees' property allegedly disappeared from the property cupboard. A recording of that room would provide a record of who had had access to the cupboard.

We suggest that:

- all rooms and corridors in the booking area should be covered by CCTV surveillance. The only exceptions would be those areas where absolute privacy is required; the forensic medical examiner's room and the interview and consultation rooms.

The cameras and property

Cameras above the booking-in desk can be a useful tool for officers when listing detainees' property. We discovered that some officers at Kilburn already chose to hold up and name, in front of the cameras, certain items as they were removed from detainees. We realise that to do this for all property would be unnecessarily time-consuming, but valuable items (such as large quantities of money) and potential evidence (such as quantities of drugs) could usefully be identified in this manner. Instigating such a policy would be an additional means of cross-checking the written property record.

We suggest that:

- the cameras behind the booking-in desk should be used to supplement the written record when valuable property or alleged evidence is removed from detainees.

Informing detainees of the cameras presence

We noted that many detainees did not realise that CCTV was operating within the custody suite. At the booking-in stage they should be told that they are under video surveillance *throughout* the custody suite and have the notices pointed out to them.

As an extra aid for those who have learning difficulties, the written signs within the custody suite should have a visual indicator showing clearly that cameras are installed. Signs should also be placed within the cells and, to avoid potential ligature points, these could be spray-painted on the wall or ceiling.

At Kilburn the cell cameras were not audio-linked, but this was not clarified in any of the signs – and was often not believed by detainees and their solicitors, even when explained. This should be made explicit in all the signs, again using an additional visual indicator.

We suggest that:

- all detainees should be told they are being monitored by CCTV throughout the custody suite – and including the cells – when they are booked in. They should also be told that the cells are not audio-linked;

- solicitors should be provided with an official description of the purposes and capabilities of the CCTV scheme, covering what it can and cannot do and how it can be used;

- there should be signs indicating the presence of cameras in both the booking areas and the cells. The written sign should have additional visual indicators that cameras are in use.

Which system? – 'open' versus 'closed'

Both systems have aspects which commend them. An 'open' system provides an evidential record and also affords the possibility of greater protection for detainees, because officers can monitor them and respond immediately should detainees need assistance. (We noted that the 'open' system could also assist officers to assess the state of a detainee prior to a visit by an FME or a cell relocation.) However, an 'open' system inevitably means loss of privacy. A 'closed' system does not affect privacy in the same way, but it offers no element of 'real time' protection for prisoners and simply becomes a retrospective record of events (still valuable to prisoners and police officers).

Balancing these, and bearing in mind that the majority of those we interviewed preferred the possibility of added protection – even while disliking the loss of privacy – we support the 'open' system already installed at Kilburn police station.

There is, however, a modification that should be considered. Officers, in informal discussions, made it clear that night-time monitoring of detainees was unsatisfactory. Under PACE *Codes of Practice* detainees are entitled to a rest period of eight hours. Most prefer to have the lights turned off. If this is done they cannot be seen by the cameras. In effect, this potentially means that up to a third of each day could be largely unrecorded by the cameras. When the 'open' system was installed the company responsible included an infra-red 'black' illumination facility which illuminates the complete cell, even though it appears to be in darkness as far as the detainee is concerned. This facility (which only works with non-coloured film) was not activated when the system started operating. The company concerned has estimated that activating it would add approximately 5 per cent to the total cost of installation. We think this would increase significantly the comfort afforded detainees without affecting the ability of the police to monitor the cameras.

We suggest that:

- an 'open' system (that is, a monitored system) provides greater protection for detainees;

- an infra-red 'black' illumination facility should be part of the 'open' system.

Should all cells have CCTV?

The PCA first recommended that 'cells for vulnerable and drunken prisoners should be equipped with cameras' in its 1996/97 Annual Report. This recommendation was amplified in 1999 with the statement that 'CCTV coverage of custody suites should be expanded to include one or two observation cells for particularly vulnerable detainees'. The PCA's recommendation is viewed by them as a starting point for debate and evaluation, rather than a fixed position.

As our research has revealed, the great majority of respondents supported an 'open' system of monitoring and the placing of cameras in all cells. They believed this combination would offer extra protection, an enhanced record of events and increased public confidence. Officers were particularly concerned that limiting the number of cells with camera surveillance would place them in an impossible position should they later be asked to justify each decision, in the face of competing claims from vulnerable detainees.

We find this one of the hardest suggestions to make, but believe that the need for privacy is, in the final analysis, outweighed by the competing claim of protection.

We suggest that:

- where a cell CCTV system is operating, all cells should have cameras installed.

Privacy and the cameras

We have shown that protection cannot be achieved without a concomitant loss of privacy. We believe that this loss of privacy can be justified precisely because of the additional gain, which is the possibility of increased protection for detainees. However, in most of the interviews we conducted the filming of the toilets consistently emerged as being of greatest concern to respondents. In attempting to balance these competing claims of privacy and protection we do not think that the loss of privacy must be absolute. It is technically possible for the toilet area to be electronically masked. The police might be concerned that detainees could harm themselves while hidden in this way, but the extent of masking can be correctly determined. Therefore, the disappearance of a detainee below the sight-line would be cause for immediate investigation of what was happening. The police might also be concerned that this private area would enable detainees to dispose of evidence, but this can already be done, despite the cameras.

We suggest that:

- as the cell cameras are primarily for purposes of protection, rather than for evidential purposes, the toilet area should be electronically masked on the monitoring screen.

Monitoring the cameras

As we know, money was not provided by the Metropolitan Police so that extra staff could be employed to monitor the cameras at Kilburn police station. In a busy custody suite it cannot realistically be expected that officers will be able to monitor CCTV screens at all times. This was recognised at Kilburn by the adoption of the Protocols, the third of which said 'there is no requirement for the custody staff to view the CCTV monitors on a constant basis'.

However, having such a Protocol immediately raises the question of how frequently cameras will be monitored. Further, will the monitoring be frequent enough to afford proper protection to detainees? Moreover, will it be sufficient for local communities to feel confident in the level of protection offered? We raise this here because if the cameras are not consistently monitored then our preceding suggestions about the balance of privacy and protection, and 'open' and 'closed' systems, are undermined. An 'open' system in all cells is hard to justify unless it is consistently monitored. We recognise that having dedicated staff to monitor the cameras is neither feasible nor economic. However, some minimum standards are required and should be made explicit in the Protocols.

We suggest that:

- a strengthened Protocol should be introduced, which advises custody staff about minimum standards of CCTV monitoring. These minimum standards should indicate to the staff how the scheme is to be run, and should indicate to the public the limitations of such surveillance;
- Protocols should be publicly available.

Cross-gender monitoring of the cameras

Considerable anxiety has been expressed by detainees about who monitors the cameras. Women detainees have felt profoundly discomforted by the knowledge that they can be viewed by staff – and, more specifically, male staff – when using the toilet. Some men have expressed similar reservations about themselves being observed. Similarly, some staff have said that they preferred not to be able to view the toilet area, even while acknowledging that the toilets can be used to dispose of evidence. There are also cultural mores to be considered. The difficulty for the police is that there are fewer women officers than there are men and, on any given shift, it can never be guaranteed that a woman will be included. For this reason we again suggest that the toilet area should be electronically masked. The alternative – providing officers with the technical ability to blank out screens while recording continues – is unsatisfactory as it does not remove the possibility that cross-gender observation of private acts will inadvertently take place.

We suggest that:

- as the cell cameras are primarily for purposes of protection, rather than for evidential purposes, the toilet area should be electronically masked on the monitoring screen.

Strip searching

Cells are also used for the strip searching of detainees. The PACE *Codes of Practice* carefully delineate how these should be conducted. A detainee must be stripped by someone of the same sex; the search should not be observed by anyone who is not required to be present; the search should normally be conducted in stages, with detainees being allowed to cover one part of their body before uncovering another. While we would prefer that all such searches should be conducted in complete privacy, we recognise that there are also issues of protection to be considered. If the cell cameras are to provide an evidential record of interaction between police and detainees it is important that they should not be used selectively. The cameras provide a safeguard both for detainees and officers against the possibility of actual and alleged improper conduct. Moreover, as this research has illustrated, the presence of cameras would appear to lead to a reduction in the use of strip searching – arguably a positive change. However, the filming and watching of strip searches is possibly the most intrusive aspect of all of the Kilburn experiment. A compromise would be to have a room/cell in which such searches were conducted that was covered by a 'closed' CCTV camera. That is, the search would be filmed and recorded, but not simultaneously watched by custody staff. The facility for doing this already exists in the system installed at Kilburn and can be activated at no extra cost.

We suggest that:

- strip searches should be monitored using a 'closed' CCTV surveillance system.

Telephoning solicitors

As the *Notice to Detained Person* stipulates, detainees may talk to solicitors *in private* (emphasis added) on the telephone. This right is more fully clarified in section C6(a) 6.1 of the *Codes of Practice*. The only telephone available to detainees is opposite the booking-in desk and fully within earshot of officers and anyone else who may be present at the time. The installation of audio-linked cameras in that same area is a further intrusion upon these supposedly 'private' conversations. We think this situation could be avoided by the provision of a sealed telephone booth for the use of detainees. If there are concerns about the safety of detainees, and the ability of officers to monitor them, such booths could incorporate plexiglas type panels.

We suggest that:

- a private telephone booth should be available for detainees wishing to consult with their solicitors. If there are concerns about safety and monitoring, then the booth could incorporate plexiglas type panels.

PACE and the Codes of Practice

Section C3.5A of the *Codes of Practice* reads, 'if video cameras are installed in the custody area, notices which indicate that cameras are in use shall be prominently displayed. Any request by a detained person or other person to have video cameras switched off shall be refused'. This section pre-dates the installation of cell cameras in police stations and should be precise in defining which parts of the 'custody area' are covered by CCTV.

We suggest that:

- section C3.5A of the PACE *Codes of Practice* should be amended so that cell cameras and their use are specifically mentioned.

As we made clear in Chapter 2, the Kilburn experiment was prompted by the untimely death of Marlon Downes in Harlesden police station. His family campaigned for the installation of CCTV in police cells so that other unexpected deaths in custody would be more readily explained than when Marlon died. In our research we wanted to consider the extent to which the circumstances of his death might have been more readily clarified had CCTV been installed in the cells on the morning of the 23 March 1997.

Having now done so, we think that the CCTV system presently in place at Kilburn police station is capable of providing answers to questions similar to those asked by the Downes family four years ago. However, as our suggestions have made clear, there are aspects of the system which need further consideration and action. If these points are not addressed, it will be harder to convince the public of the integrity of a system which was launched to 'allow for complete transparency of police treatment of prisoners, enhance prisoner care and improve community confidence in Brent Police' (*The Job*, 24 March 2000). Those working, detained and assisting at Kilburn police station have, through their individual comments, shown how a more effective scheme may be implemented.

Notes

1 *Installation of CCTV in custody cells at Kilburn Operational Command Unit* December 1998.

Appendix

Kilburn Cell-based CCTV system

The purpose of the system is to enhance prisoner care and increase public confidence in the police care of persons detained.

Protocols

1. The custody officer is responsible for the care and protection of prisoners. This equally applies to those officers relieving the custody officer.
2. The CCTV system must not act as a replacement to the normal methods of prisoner care already in place e.g. visits, observation, etc. The CCTV system is to enhance the care already available.
3. There is no requirement for the custody staff to view the CCTV monitors on a constant basis.
4. Custody officers must complete the risk assessment form in all cases (Per Form 1).
5. Mental assessment of prisoners by FMEs and qualified psychiatric teams may be assisted by access to the monitors and where appropriate should be permitted.
6. The custody officer is responsible for the integrity of the CCTV system.
7. The multiplex screen should be used to monitor all cells and detention rooms. The small screen should be used to view those detained whose demeanour causes concern or is otherwise worthy of closer monitoring.
8. It is the custody officer's responsibility to ensure that voyeurism is

not allowed under any circumstances.

9 The CCTV tapes may be used to provide evidence in any criminal or internal proceedings.

10 Where evidence is obtained in view of cameras, this must be noted on case papers under disclosure form MG6C.

11 Lay visitors will not be allowed access to the monitors or tapes.

12 The tapes will only be viewed by lay panels on the authority of the OCU [Operational Command Unit] Commander in order to prevent serious public disorder.

13 The custody officer has responsibility to ensure that the CCTV tapes are changed as required.

14 All CCTV tapes are to be sealed in accordance with instructions and recorded in Book 105.

15 No CCTV tapes covering the cells are to be viewed without the authority of the Chief Inspector CJU [Criminal Justice Unit].

Bibliography

Association of Metropolitan Authorities (AMA) (1990) *Crime Reduction – A Framework for the 1990s*. London: AMA.

Bannister, J., Fyfe, N.R. and Kearns, A. (1998) Closed circuit television and the city, in C. Norris, J. Morgan and G. Armstrong (eds) *Surveillance, Closed Circuit Television and Social Control*. Aldershot: Ashgate.

Bauman, Z. (1998) *Freedom*. Milton Keynes: Open University Press.

Bauman, Z. (1999) *In Search of Politics*. Cambridge: Polity Press.

Bauman, Z. (2000) *Liquid Modernity*. Cambridge: Polity Press.

Benn, M. and Worpole, K. (1986) *Death in the City: An examination of police-related deaths in London*. London: Canary Press.

Bottomley, K., Coleman, C., Dixon, D., Gill, M. and Wall, D. (1989) *The Impact of Aspects of the Police and Criminal Evidence Act 1984 on Policing in a Force in the North of England*, Final Report to the ESRC, unpublished.

Brown, D. (1989) *Detention at the police station under the Police and Criminal Evidence Act 1984*, Home Office Research Study No. 104. London: HMSO.

Brown, D. (1997) *PACE ten years on: a review of the research*, Home Office Research Study No. 155. London: Home Office.

Brown, D. and Bucke, T. (1997) *In Police Custody: Police powers and suspects rights under the revised PACE Codes of Practice*, Home Office Research Study 174. London: Home Office.

Brown, D., Ellis, T. and Larcombe, K. (1992) *Changing the Code: Police detention under the revised PACE Codes of Practice*, Home Office Research Study No. 35. London: HMSO.

Bucke, T. and Brown, D. (1997) *In Police Custody: Police powers and suspects rights under the revised PACE Codes of Practice*, Home Office Research Study 174. London: Home Office.

Burrows, J. (1979) The impact of closed circuit television on crime in the

London Underground, in P. Mayhew, R. Clarke, J. Burrows, M. Hough and S. Winchester (eds) *Crime in the Public View*. London: HMSO.

Chesney-Lind, M. (1997) *The Female Offender: Girls, women and crime*. Thousand Oaks, CA: Sage.

Cohen, S. (1985) *Visions of Social Control*. Cambridge: Polity Press.

Crawford, A. (1997) *The Local Governance of Crime: Appeals to community and partnerships*. Oxford: Clarendon Press.

Davies, S.G. (1998) CCTV: A new battleground for privacy, in C. Norris, J. Morgan and G. Armstrong (eds) *Surveillance, Closed Circuit Television and Social Control*. Aldershot: Ashgate.

Davis, M. (1998) *Ecology of Fear: Los Angeles and the imagination of disaster*. New York: Henry Holt.

Department for Education and Employment (DfEE) (2001) *Skills for Life*. London: The Stationery Office.

Devon and Cornwall Constabulary (2000) *In-cell monitoring – Analysis of the pilot at the Exeter Custody Unit*, Unpublished report, Criminal Justice and Operational Support Division, Devon and Cornwall Constabulary.

De Waard, J. (1999) The private security industry in international perspective, *European Journal on Criminal Policy and Research* 7(2), 143–74.

Dixon, D. (1990) Juvenile suspects and the Police and Criminal Evidence Act, in D. Freestone (ed.) *Children and the Law: Essays in honour of Professor H.K. Bevan*. Hull: Hull University Press.

Dixon, D. (1991) Common sense, legal advice and the right of silence, *Public Law*, 233–54.

Dixon, D. (1992) Legal regulation and policing practice, *Social and Legal Studies*, 1, 515–41.

Dixon, D., Bottomley, A.K. Coleman, C., Gill, M. and Wall, D. (1990) Safeguarding the rights of suspects in police custody, *Policing and Society*, 1, 115–40.

Elias, N. (1978) *The Civilizing Process: The history of manners*. Oxford: Basil Blackwell.

Elias, N. (1982) *State Formation and Civilization: The civilizing process*. Oxford: Basil Blackwell.

Ericson, R.V. and Haggerty, K.D. (1997) *Policing the Risk Society*. Oxford: Clarendon.

Evans, R. (1993) *The Conduct of Police Interviews with Juveniles*, Royal Commission on Criminal Justice Research Study No. 8. London: HMSO.

Evans, R. and Rawsthorne, S. (1994) *The Protection of Vulnerable Suspects*, A report to the Home Office Research and Planning Unit, Unpublished.

Foucault, M. (1977) *Discipline and Punish*. Harmondsworth: Penguin.

Fox, R.G. (2001) Someone to Watch Over Us: Back to the panopticon? *Criminal Justice*, **1**, 3.

Fyfe, N.R. and Bannister, J. (1996) City Watching: Closed circuit television in public spaces, *Area*, **28**(1), 37–46.

Garland, D. (1996) The limits of the sovereign state: Strategies of crime control in contemporary society, *British Journal of Criminology*, **36**(4), 445–71.

Garland, D. (2001) *The Culture of Control*. Oxford: Oxford University Press.

Giddens, A. (1985) *The Nation State and Violence: Volume Two of a contemporary critique of historical materialism*. Cambridge: Polity Press.

Graham, S. (1998) Towards the fifth utility? On the extension and normalisation of public CCTV, in C. Norris, J. Morgan and G. Armstrong (eds) *Surveillance, Closed Circuit Television and Social Control*. Aldershot: Ashgate.

Graham, S., Brooks, J. and Heery, D. (1996) Towns on the television: CCTV in British towns and cities, *Local Government Studies*, **22**(3), 3–27.

Honess, T. and Charman, E. (1992) *Closed circuit television in public places: Its acceptability and perceived effectiveness*, Crime Prevention Unit Paper 35. London: Home Office.

Jacobs, J. (1961) *The Death and Life of Great American Cities*. New York: Vintage.

Johnston, L. (2000) *Policing Britain: Risk, security and governance*. Harlow: Longman.

Jones, R. (2000) Digital Rule: punishment, control and technology. *Punishment and Society*, **2**(1), 5–22.

Jones, T. and Newburn, T., (1998) *Private Security and Public Policing*. Oxford: Clarendon Press.

Judge, T. (1986) The provisions in practice, in J. Benyon and C. Bourn (eds) *The Police: Powers, procedures and proprieties*. Oxford: Pergamon Press.

Justice (1998) *Under Surveillance*. London: Justice.

Lash, S. (2000) *Technologies of life*, Inaugural Lecture, Goldsmiths College, University of London.

Leigh, A., Johnson, G. and Ingram, A. (1998) *Deaths in Police Custody: Learning the lessons*, Police Research Series Paper 26. London: Home Office.

Lyon, D. (1994) *The Electronic Eye: The rise of surveillance society*. Cambridge: Polity Press.

Lyon, D. (2001) *Surveillance Society: Monitoring everyday life*. Buckingham: Open University Press.

McConville, M., Sanders, A. and Leng, R. (1991) *The Case for the Prosecution*. London: Routledge.

Manning, P.K. (1983) *Police Work: the social organization of policing*. Cambridge, MA: MIT Press.

Marx, G. (1998) *Undercover: Police Surveillance in America*. Berkeley: University of California Press.

Metropolitan Police (1997) *Evaluation of the Video Recording Systems in the Custody Suites at Brixton, Vauxhall and Streatham*, Unpublished report, Consultancy and Information Services, Metropolitan Police.

Metropolitan Police (2001) *Draft Policy: Video and audio recording and the custody suite area*.

Morgan, R. (1996) Custody in the police station: How do England and Wales measure up in Europe? *Policy Studies*, **17**(1), 55–7.

Newburn, T. (2001) The Introduction of CCTV into a Custody Suite: Some reflections on risk, surveillance and policing, in A. Crawford (ed.) *Safety and Insecurity in the New Millennium*. Cullompton: Willan Publishing.

Norris, C., Moran, J., and Armstrong, G. (eds) (1998) *Surveillance, Closed Circuit Television and Social Control*. Aldershot, Ashgate.

Palmer, C. (1996) The appropriate adult, *Legal Action*, May.

Police Complaints Authority (PCA) (1997) *Annual Report*. London: The Stationery Office.

Police Complaints Authority (PCA) (1998) *Annual Report*. London: The Stationery Office.

Police Complaints Authority (PCA) (1999) *Deaths in Police Custody: Reducing the risks*. London: Police Complaints Authority.

Police Complaints Authority (PCA) (2000) *One Year On. Deaths in Police Custody: Reducing the risks*. London: Police Complaints Authority.

Poyner, B. (1988) Video cameras and bus vandalism, *Journal of Security and Administration*, **11**, 44–51.

Poyner, B. (1992) Situational crime prevention in two parking facilities, in R. Clarke (ed.) *Situational Crime Prevention: Successful case studies*. New York: Harrow and Heston.

Reiner, R. (2000) *The Politics of the Police*, third edition. Oxford: Oxford University Press.

Reiss, A. (1987) The legitimacy of intrusion into private spaces, in C. Shearing and P. Stenning (eds) *Private Policing*. Beverly Hills: Sage.

Robertson, G. (1992) *The Role of Police Surgeons*, Royal Commission on Criminal Justice Research Study No. 6. London: HMSO.

Rose, D. (1996) *In the Name of the Law*. London: Verso.

Rose, N. (1999) *Powers of Freedom: Reframing political thought*. Cambridge: Cambridge University Press.

Royal Commission on Criminal Justice (RCCJ) (1993) *Report*. London: HMSO.

Royal Commission on Criminal Procedure (RCCP) (1981) *Report*. London: HMSO.

Sanders, A. (1997) From suspect to trial, in M. Maguire, R. Morgan and R. Reiner (eds) *The Oxford Handbook of Criminology*. Oxford: Clarendon Press.

Savage, S., Moon, G., Kelly, K. and Bradshaw, Y. (1997) Divided loyalties? – The police surgeon and criminal justice, *Policing and Society*, 2, 82.

Scraton, P. and Chadwick, K. (1987a) *In the Arms of the Law: Coroner's inquests and deaths in custody*. London: Pluto Press.

Scraton, P. and Chadwick, K. (1987b) Speaking ill of the dead: Institutionalized responses to deaths in custody, in P. Scraton (ed.) *Law, Order and the Authoritarian State*. Milton Keynes: Open University Press.

Shaw, M. (1999) A video camera can change your life, in S. Cook and S. Davies (eds) *Harsh Punishment*. Boston: Northeastern University Press.

Shaw, S. (1999) The CPT's visits to the United Kingdom, in R. Morgan and M. Evans (eds) *Protecting Prisoners*. Oxford: Oxford University Press.

Shearing C. and Stenning P. (1981) Modern private security: Its growth and implications, In M. Tonry and N. Morris (eds) *Crime and Justice: An Annual Review of Research*. Chicago: University of Chicago Press.

Smith, G. (1999) The Butler Report: An opportunity missed? *New Law Journal* 20 August.

Standing Conference on Crime Prevention (1991) *Safer Communities: The local delivery of crime prevention through the partnership approach*. London: Home Office.

Stern, V. (1989) *Bricks of Shame: Britain's prisons*, second edition. Harmondsworth: Penguin.

Tilley, N. (1998) Evaluating the effectiveness of CCTV schemes, in C. Norris, J. Morgan and G. Armstrong (eds) *Surveillance, Closed Circuit Television and Social Control*. Aldershot: Ashgate.

Tyler, T. (1990) *Why People Obey the Law*. New Haven: Yale University Press.

Weatheritt, M. and Vieira, C. (1998) *Lay Visiting to Police Stations*, Home Office Research Study 188. London: Home Office.

Whittington, R. (1998) The coroner's inquiry, in A. Leibling (ed.) *Deaths of*

Offenders: The hidden side of justice. Winchester: Waterside Press.

Williams, K.S. and Johnstone, C. (2000) The politics of the selective gaze: Closed circuit television and the policing of public space, *Crime, Law and Social Change*, **34**(2), 183–210.

Willis, C.F. (1984) *The Tape-recording of Police Interviews with Suspects*, Home Office Research Study No. 82. London: HMSO.

Willis, C.F., Macleod, J. and Naish, P. (1988) *The Tape-recording of Police Interviews with Suspects: A second interim report*, Home Office Research Study No. 97. London HMSO.

Young, J. (1999) *The Exclusive Society*. London: Sage.

Index

Added to a page number, f denotes a figure, t denotes a table.